The Mending Basket
Stitching Hope When Life Unravels

By

Margaret T. Jensen

Dedication

Dedicated to Dr. Judson Carlberg, President of Gordon College; and Janice Dawn Carlberg, Gordon's First Lady, and First Lady in the hearts of her family.

In 1982, Jan & Jud gave me a special gift — a ticket to Gordon's Writers' Conference. There I met Les Stobbe, who published my first book, *First We Have Coffee*, with Here's Life Publisher.

Not only is Judson Carlberg an outstanding administrator, but he is also a loving husband to my daughter Jan. He is a devoted father and grandfather —also a thoughtful and encouraging son-in-law to me.

Jan and Jud work as a team as they continue to stitch hope into a broken world through Gordon students "going into all the world" with a Biblical World View, bringing hope and healing through God's redeeming love — John 3:16.

Thank You!

Gordon College
255 Grapevine Road
Wenham, Mass.

Janice & Jud Carlberg

Acknowledgements

Thank you, Olivia and Jim Michaels, for your unwavering faith and labor of love to publish *The Mending Basket* through "Carolina Times Magazine."

Thank you, Jean Bryant, for your labor of love in editing my books.

Thank you, Sarah, for organizing my albums — we turned it into a story.

There are not enough words to express my heart's gratitude to my beloved family and friends, across the ocean and at home, for stitching hope with multicolored yarn.

Thank you, Wilmington Printing Company, for adding *The Mending Basket* to your busy schedule.

Thank you, John and Rene' of Braswell Photography, for the beautiful cover for *The Mending Basket*.

Thank you, Elizabeth Norton, for the layout / design of the book.

God, the Master Weaver, turns what we cannot see into a pattern of beauty.

God bless you all and keep you in His loving care. Thank you for your love and prayers.

— Margaret Jensen

Quotations from:

The King James Version Bible

Streams in the Desert, Cowman

My Utmost for His Highest, Oswald Chambers

Distilled Wisdom, compiled and edited by
        Alfred Armond Montapert

With the Word, Warren Wiersbe

Endorsements for *The Mending Basket*

―――≫・o・≪―――

"Margaret Jensen has spent eight decades mending hearts of stranger and family alike. We have had the privilege of watching Margaret's life for over thirty years. Her heartrending and often humorous stories span five generations, bringing wisdom, insight and truths that last. You'll find *Mending* will stitch much needed hope securely to your heart."
— *Gordon and Gail MacDonald*

"Hope is enjoying the things of God's tomorrow today. And nobody lives or writes it better than Margaret Jensen. While I have had the privilege of being her pastor, now I find she is mine. Her stories live in my soul. They light my path in Christ. My wife and I have enjoyed many evenings around her supper table. And her stories, as much as her sumptuous meals, are bread for life."
— *The Rev. Stephen M. Crotts, Presbyterian Minister, Director, The Carolina Study Center*

"Engaging and real, Margaret Jensen has developed a fan club of listeners from around the country. She has endeared herself to them through real-life stories that help us smile, laugh, cry and regain new focus, so that even during the 'dark days, we recall God's goodness and understand His love. A few minutes of upbeat warmth and sparkle with Margaret Jensen deliver a boost to one's spirit and help grab new hope for today."
— *Jim Warren, Retired Host of Prime Time America*

"Margaret Jensen! Margaret Jensen exudes inspiration. One does not read her writing, sip coffee with her or attend one of her speaking engagements without absorbing her spiritual vitality, her insightful grasp of life. Simple stories come alive. You laugh, you cry. Subtle lessons for living move you toward the Lord she loves. Margaret's craft with words is truly God's gift to us all."
— *Eldred Nelson*

"How I love the title *The Mending Basket*! It reminds me of Mother's sewing basket 70 years ago. It is good to see a title that isn't artificial, one that flows with values and hope. Yes, Margaret's writing makes a huge difference."
— *Oscar Greene, Guideposts devotional writer*

"Margaret Jensen is a national treasure whose writing never fails to enrich and entertain me. A gifted storyteller with a rare blend of heart and humor, Margaret continues to weave the old and the new together and help us draw closer to God. I thank God that I live in this day when she is sharing her happy wisdom so lavishly."
— *Warren W. Wiersbe, Author and Bible Teacher*

"Margaret Jensen can give an earthly event a potent heavenly meaning faster than anyone I know. While others may complain about a negative event, Margaret will reveal God's truth oozing from the experience. Her stories do not only stir you intellectually, however, for they hook themselves in your heart so the heavenly truth can be applied when a life experience matches that in the story."
— *Les Stobbe, Literary Agent*

The Mending Basket

Table of Contents

Preface

When I talked with the family after September 11, 2001, and asked, "How do we prepare for tragedy — like Ground Zero — in our lives?" Chris, Ralph's wife and my daughter-in-law, answered, "Mom, we do just what we are doing—keep the traditions, hold the family together and face whatever comes with God's grace."

I began writing what we were doing while going back to remember the yesterdays that bring hope for today — the hope that is the anchor of the soul for the tomorrows.

Hope springs up between the cracks of our doubts like a flower coming up through the crack in my patio.

— Margaret Jensen

Introduction

The Master Weaver 1878

My ordinary day, filled with multiple, mundane memos was suddenly changed into a molten moment.

In my hand I held a special delivery package from Norway.

My runaway train of tedious tasks was turned back to yesterday, 1878.

Before me was a copy of a work of art that revealed beautifully embroidered stitches that wove eternal truths from yesterday into today and tomorrow.

"Congratulations on your Confirmation"

"May the Almighty God protect and guide you, my beloved daughters, and direct you in all your ways." 1878

I held the lengthy Norwegian message before me and recalled the stories of broken hearts and hopeless dreams. Yet, through the tangled yarn of joy and sorrow, the Master Weaver stitched hope from generation to generation with eternal truths that never change.

"Remember that from a child you have been taught that Salvation is through Jesus Christ." (II Timothy 3:14,15)

Read Psalms 51:1: "Where there is a plea for mercy and forgiveness."

I reached for my Bible to read the suggested passage — Psalms 25.

From the embroidered thread my "independent" great grandmother Amelia was stitching hope to my grandmother, Bertilda, on her Confirmation day. That thread was woven into the heart of my godly Mama and will continue to bring future generations to the heart of God from the prayers that have gone before us.

I read, Psalm 25

"Oh God, I trust in Thee"
"Show me Thy ways"
"Lead me into Truth"
"The secret of the Lord is with them that fear Him and He will show them His covenant."

Through many dangers, toils and snares we have already come — and it is Amazing Grace that brings us safely Home.

Joyce and I are alone now. Grace, Gordon, Doris, Jeanelle, Bernice are singing our song. Today, our verse is Psalm 71:18: "show Thy strength to this generation and Thy powers to every one that is to come."

"May those who come behind us find us faithful."

Thank you for the gift, Cousin Marit.

— Your American Cousins, Joyce & Margaret.

Now also when I am old and grayheaded,
O God do not forsake me
Until I declare your strength to this generation
You power to everyone
who is to come.

Chapter One

Beacon of Faith

Hurricane winds swept over the sandy shores of Wrightsville Beach, North Carolina, then came roaring like a runaway freight train through the woods in back of my house. Hurricane Fran, 1996, made its debut with a fury.

With a splintering crash the mighty Live Oak bent slowly as though reluctant to leave the throne as "King of the Forest." Pine trees crackling under the force of the wind sounded like gunfire in a battle zone. Since Ralph, my son, lived near Masonboro Sound, evacuation was in order; so he came with his wife, Chris, and their children, Shawn, Eric, Sarah and Kathryn Elise, to my safe house in town.

It was a reminder of a Garrison Keillor story about Minnesota storms and rural children in school who were assigned a safe house in town when winter blizzards made farm roads impassable.

Everyone needs a safe house, not only from physical storms, but the winds that shatter the soul.

Huddled under blankets, we waited for daybreak to view the storm's path of destruction.

When I reached for the coffee pot, I heard the screeching brakes of a car in the driveway. "That has to be Chad." It was! My daughter, Janice, married to Dr. Judson Carlberg, President of Gordon College, has two children, Heather and Chad.

After graduation from Gordon College, Wenham, Massachusetts, Chad desired the adventure of doing everything he wanted to do: art, children's theater, acting and writing.

"I'm coming to Wilmington, Grammy."

He came! "All of life's a stage" and my creative grandson played his part with a zest for living and a spontaneous humor that made a rainy day look like sunshine. He likes nothing better than to remind his cousin Shawn (six months younger) that he, Chad, is "Number One Grandson!"

Through the back door he burst forth with, "It was awesome! Man, oh man, the crash was horrendous; the storm kept us in my art studio all night. We couldn't see anything until the morning. You wouldn't believe the sound! It was the steeple of the First Baptist Church! The steeple fell. People came from everywhere, but the pastor said, 'The steeple fell; the church stands.' It was awesome!"

"Ah, that coffee smells good and the pancakes." Everyone sat around the table in the breakfast room and Ralph paused to give thanks to God for His protection and provision; then the conversation continued.

"That steeple, 197 feet tall, stood for 130 years," Ralph said. "Through the turmoil of hurricanes, economics and cultural storms, it was a beacon of faith and a monument of tenacity."

In the background, the bacon sizzled in the pan, the coffee perked and I took orders for Norwegian pancakes, rolled in homemade syrup and sprinkled with powdered sugar.

"The steeple will rise again!"

"Remember the tree house Papa helped us build in that powerful Live Oak tree? Well, Chad, it crashed last night, and the tree house with it. I still have the carpenter's apron Papa gave me," Shawn added wistfully.

The grandchildren missed their Papa who went Home in 1991, but we live with cherished memories.

"No one is really gone when memories are alive," I thought to myself.

"Uncle Ralph, how could that mighty oak crash? It stood so

many years through so many storms."

The conversation flowed while the pancakes made the rounds.

"There was a time when the Live Oaks were called Royal Oaks because the wood was used in ships for the King," Ralph continued between cups of coffee. "The strength of the joints or crotch, that angle formed by two limbs, was a most important part, the strength in ship building. It wasn't only the wind that felled the tree, but the deluge of rain that soaked the ground around the roots. That powerful tree was uprooted by water and toppled by the wind."

I listened to the cacophony of sound, mingling voices around the table, the dog barking at the squirrels, saws buzzing in competition all along the street — all blending in discordant notes like tuning up for a concert.

It was a "tune-up" for the symphony of life.

My thoughts were interrupted when Ralph said it was time to check on their neighborhood at Masonboro Sound and see how the furniture factory had withstood the storm.

The cars pulled out of the driveway and I sat alone with my cup of coffee. I reached for my Bible and read that, "we are trees of righteousness, the planting of the Lord, that He might be glorified." (Isaiah 61:3).

I reached for my worn devotional book, *Streams in the Desert*, a gift from Eleanor Holby for my sixteenth birthday, 1932, and turned the pages yellow with age to January 16, and read:

> *There is no storm hath power to blast the tree*
> *God knows;*
> *no thunderbolt, nor beating rain, nor lightening*
> *flash nor hurricane;*
> *when they are spent, it doth remain the tree God*
> *knows,*
> *through every tempest standeth fast, and from its*
> *first day to its last, still fairer grows.*
>
> — *Streams in the Desert* (selected)
> Compiled by Mrs. Charles Cowman

It was the day of Hurricane Fran, 1996.
A tree will grow again.
The steeple will rise.
The church stands, a beacon of faith and
a promise of hope.

— M.T.J.

. . . .

On another day, we stood on the patio and watched the sun splashed waves crash against the rocky shore of Gloucester, Massachusetts.

Since the President's home, Wilson House, was in the process of renovation, Jan and Jud had brought their guests from Norway to the condominium at Gloucester, and the Nelsons from Seattle had joined me. I had come from Wilmington, North Carolina, to welcome our mutual friends from Oslo.

On this bright morning, we watched the ocean. We set the table on the patio for a Norwegian breakfast: hard rolls, a platter of sliced cheese, rolled up ham, herring in wine sauce, fruit, and the coffeepot perked happily.

"What a beautiful sight; the rocky coast much like Norway," Bjorne Langmo exclaimed to Eldred Nelson.

"Today Jan will pick us up for a grand tour of the New England coast."

"Don't forget the outlets," Ruth Nelson added.

"*O ja,* women have to shop and that goes for my *Rut* (Ruth). Then we will find some famous seafood places especially known for lobster."

The coffee cups were refilled and conversation flowed about plans for cameras and sweaters ready for a tour of beautiful New England.

A call came!

"Turn on the T.V.!"

We stood with our cameras and walking shoes, motionless

with disbelief as the horror of the "Day of Infamy" rolled before our eyes. It was September 11, 2001.

"I'm on my way to get you," Jan called. "Jud has opened the chapel to the students and community."

Silently we slipped into the van — there were no words for our thoughts.

As we drove onto the Gordon College campus we watched students, arms around each other moving silently toward the chapel. Unaware of looking like tourists, we slipped quietly into the second row and watched Dr. Carlberg and the faculty move into the front row. The sound of awesome silence filled the chapel: silent tears, unspoken sighing prayers and unheard cries from deep within the soul that called for answers.

Out of the quiet, the organist sat down and from the majestic roll of the organ came an old hymn from the 1600s.

Be still my soul, thy God doth undertake
to guide the future as He has the past.
Thy hope, thy confidence let nothing shake;
all new mysteries shall be bright at last.
Be still my soul; the waves and winds still know
His voice who ruled them while He dwelt below.

The blazing Towers, the crash of glass and steel, the cries of fleeing people, the screams of sirens. Suddenly, the images we saw with our eyes were now stilled by what we knew by faith. "Be still my soul!"

Soft like the voice of an angel came the whispers of hope, and we heard another sound from the organ:

I need Thee, O I need Thee
Every hour I need Thee
O bless me now my Savior
I come to Thee.

From the back roads of my mind, a memory from a long ago time, as a child in Papa's Norwegian church in Chicago, came the sound of the immigrants singing, "I need Thee, O I need Thee" with a thick Norwegian accent. In the midst of a changing world, the church sang.

During the depression, when we ate potatoes fried in lard, my Norwegian Mama sang and gave thanks.

> *Be not dismayed whate're betide.*
> *God will take care of you.*

We heard Mama sing! We believed! The blessings of the past rekindled faith for today and hope for tomorrow.

Hope springs up, like a blade of grass through the cracks in my driveway, and dares us to believe tomorrow will be bright.

Dr. Tom Brooks mounted the platform to announce a hymn.

I had watched him walk on stage before, handsome in his tuxedo, and he would turn to wield his baton for the orchestra and the Gordon College choral group, all in tuxedos and long black dresses, gala events in the life of the community.

Today the choral group was before him, not in tuxedos or long dresses, but in blue jeans and sweatshirts with upturned tear-stained faces. With the confidence of, not only a seasoned performer, but also of a seasoned faith, he led the choral group before him:

> *Great is Thy faithfulness,*
> *summer and winter,*
> *springtime and harvest*
> *Great is Thy faithfulness*
> *O God to us.*

The choral group was before Dr. Brooks but the audience included a host of unseen witnesses who surround us from heaven's auditorium. When God's people sing, the angels fold their wings to listen.

All those witnesses? "Through many dangers, toils and snares they had already come," and they heard us sing and when they heard us sing, "Great is Thy faithfulness! Great is Thy faithfulness O God our Father," I'm sure they joined in. (I think I heard Harold singing tenor!)

The symphony of faith winged its way to heaven.

When Dr. Carlberg said, "This day has changed our lives forever," we knew it was true. From faculty and students came public and private prayer. The open Bible proclaimed God's words of comfort and hope to breaking hearts.

> *"Fear thou not, for I am with thee. Be not dismayed for I am thy God. I will strengthen thee, and uphold thee with the right hand of my righteousness."*
>
> — Isaiah 41:10

> *"God is our refuge and strength, a very present help in time of trouble."*
>
> — Psalm 46:1

> *"I will never leave thee nor forsake thee."*
>
> — Hebrew 13:5

> *The truth that we knew in our hearts would enable us to live above and beyond the horror we have seen with our eyes. Faith is the victory!*

It was September 11, 2001; the day the monument to power and to man's creative genius fell, not by the winds of nature's hurricanes, but by the winds of hatred lashed with fury at a free world. The Towers fell! A nation stood! The church sang! Amazing Grace!

Chapter Two

Sunday Dinner

During a conversation with a college student, a young man said, "Our generation has been put out to pasture without any fences. We'd probably jump the fence but at least there would be something firm to come back to." Traditions are like fences, something to come back to when the world turns in tumultuous turmoil.

Sunday dinner is a firm place for our family to gather when stumbling steps grope for guidance. It goes beyond human understanding that the intensity of hate against a free world could motivate suicide bombers to fly into the citadel of world power. Forever etched on life's canvas will remain a picture of blazing towers, against a New York skyline, tumbling to the ground.

The morning began like any ordinary day: a cup of coffee, a goodbye kiss, then off to work. Today thousands will never have that routine morning again.

Todd Beamer's, "Let's Roll," turned ordinary people into extraordinary heroes when a hijacked plane was diverted from the intended mission of hate. On a field of green Pennsylvania, our heroes gave their today that America could have a tomorrow. The heart of a nation remembers!

For a moment in time, the empty glitz of glamour stayed backstage while the drama of reality had top billing on the stage of life called "Ground Zero."

The Actors were our neighbors next door — the firefighter who rescued grandma's kitten from a tree, or cradled a baby from a burning building; the policeman who gave me a ticket (I deserved it) or held a drug dealer at bay; the same cops on the beat who stop at *Dunkin' Donuts* for a cup of coffee; rescue workers who answer 911 and get grandpa to the emergency room, or deliver a baby who makes an early entrance.

In the tragedy played before us some cry, "Where is God?"

God was there all the time at Ground Zero, His life reflected through the men and women who dashed into a burning inferno to rescue people they didn't know. They died with arms around each other and never had time to say "goodbye" or "thank you."

In homes around the world, the stories must be told so we will never forget that the heroes were our neighbors.

We heard of co-workers who refused to leave the helpless, or passed up cold water for a burning throat because someone might need it.

A dog was told to stay. He stayed. A fireman found him and cradled him in his arms, then buried him in a safe place.

The men tipped their hats! Heroes are Heroes!

A world mourned with tears over empty hearths and lonely hearts.

Some years ago a young boy, severely burned, said, "I am alive and that's enough for me." Today, many who are still healing from severe wounds tell the world that life is a precious gift. The unborn agree!!

· · · · · · ·

After miles of travel I was home, and now it was my turn for Sunday dinner. When I am gone, Ralph and Chris open their home for family and friends to gather around their beautiful table.

There is healing in the mundane routine of living. I had returned home to the splendor of the ordinary.

Saturday night I set the table in the dining room for ten; the round table, crafted by Ralph, waits in the breakfast room for the overflow of guests.

I keep the menu simple and vary between roast beef, turkey breast or ham; the usual mashed potatoes, green beans, corn on the cob, applesauce or cranberries, and Chris' favorite, cucumbers and onions in vinegar and sugar; and I can't forget the chocolate cake for Eric.

Chris and Jan can try the gourmet recipes; I'll just stick to what I can do in my sleep.

Routine is a great stress reliever. With Lawrence Welk on Saturday night television, I can tap my foot and snap beans at the same time.

Before my 7:00 a.m. cup of coffee on Sunday morning, I put a floured and well-seasoned roast in the oven at 350°, then reach for my *Apple Annie's* coffee cake and my cup of coffee. (When Jan comes I bake pecan rolls.)

I'm sitting quietly, in a peaceful aloneness, even while missing the ones I have loved long and well.

With coffee cup in hand, the roast sizzling in the oven, I recall another day in a long ago time, Sunday dinner.

· · · · · · ·

It was 5:30 a.m. on a cold Chicago Sunday morning in a second floor flat when Papa, in his long flannel nightshirt, shook the stove. What a luxurious moment to snuggle with my two sisters, Doris and Grace, under Mama's homemade quilt, to await the warm kitchen and the aroma from Mama's coffee pot.

The night before we helped Mama set the table for Sunday dinner and peeled the potatoes and carrots (placed in cold salt water overnight), to be cooked in the morning when Mama added peas to the carrots and made a cream sauce sprinkled with parsley.

Carefully kneading the priceless ground beef (two pounds for $0.25), my Norwegian Mama added plenty of bread crumbs, chopped onions, salt and pepper and 1/4 teaspoon of allspice, then placed the meat in the icebox for Sunday morning, when she would form round balls and then brown slowly in hot grease.

When we asked her for her secret, she smiled, "*O ja*, the secret is to brown the meatballs well, then make good brown gravy using vegetable water, then let the meatballs simmer for an hour or less." Seventy-five years later it is still the family's favorite dish.

In a day when we are urged to move ahead, I seem to desire to push my boat against the current to go back to a time when life was simple, but as Mama said, "*O ja*, simple it was, but easy it was not."

We go back to remember the blessings of yesterday in order to renew our faith for today and kindle hope for tomorrow.

When we dared to peek in the icebox, it was to make sure that the best delight was there, the red quivering Jell-O! Life was good.

The clip-clop hoof beats of the horse pulling the milk wagon sounded the dawn coming through a Chicago alley. On Sunday morning it was quiet. Two bottles had been left on Saturday.

After our Saturday night bath, we laid out our clothes for Sunday morning while Papa polished seven pairs of shoes. Before falling asleep, we heard Mama and Papa enjoying a quiet cup of coffee with a sugar lump.

With the dawn of a new day, we heard Papa singing, "Early now on Sunday morning, we lift our songs of praise."

The shaking of the stove, Papa's singing and Mama's coffee pot were as routine as the dawn.

Dressed in his swallowtail coat, striped trousers and high starched collar, Papa marched off to church with Bible in hand and coattails blowing in the wind.

We walked to Sunday School in starched dresses, made from the contents of the missionary barrel, with our brother, Gordon, in a suit made from an old coat, a penny tied in the corner of our handkerchieves.

Sitting in a row with Mama, we watched in awe as Papa announced the opening hymn:

> *Praise to the Lord, the Almighty,*
> *the King of creation!*
> *O my soul praise Him,*
> *For He is thy health and salvation!*
> *All ye who hear now to His temple draw near;*
> *Join me in glad adoration.*
>
> — Joachin, 1680

We sang in Norwegian then; now, 75 years later, I sing the same great hymn in English.

After church we wondered whom Papa would invite this time.

"Come, come, *o ja*, you must come home for Mama's Sunday dinner."

Mama believed that if Jesus could handle the feeding of 5,000 with bread and fish, He could certainly multiply meatballs for Papa's guests.

Around the table, the conversation flowed (mostly from Papa), stories of faith mixed with humorous tales of trolls and fairies from past generations.

This was the time when the cares of the world were forgotten. The week before held meals of oatmeal, soup and bread and fried bologna, but today was the magic of red Jell-O with whipped cream. Life was good! We were rich!

· · · · · · ·

It was time to come back to the present, check the roast and reduce the oven to 250° and turn off the potatoes and carrots.

When I met the family at church, we sat in a row to worship together. At the close, Ralph whispered, "I invited some new people for dinner, okay?"

"Okay."

Later I heard the sounds of happy voices as cars rolled into the driveway; then the familiar orders: "Katie Elise, mash the potatoes!" "Shawn get the chairs." "Ralph, please slice the roast!" "Mom, it fell apart!" Chris filled the glasses with ice tea while I made the gravy and heated the rolls.

Since we were twelve, no one wanted to sit in the breakfast rooms. We squeezed in and joined hands for prayer. The blessing was short and sweet.

Two years old, Gracynne, Eric and Clover's daughter, and Ralph and Chris's first grandchild and my great granddaughter, sat in her high chair and shouted "Amen!"

Just as in the long ago, the stories flowed around the table while the roast and mashed potatoes made the rounds.

Looking around the table were Ralph's four children, Sarah, Kathryn Elise, Shawn and Eric and his wife, Clover, and Gracynne and guests.

Across the miles, Jan and her family would be around their Sunday dinner table, but our hearts would be together.

I told about our special friends, Gordon and Gail MacDonald, working long hours at Ground Zero.

"What did they do?"

"I know what they didn't do. As gifted as they are in expounding the Scripture and organizing Bible studies, that is not what they did, but did what was in their hand. They poured soothing drops into burning eyes, rubbed lotion on bruised hands and poured love and prayer into broken hearts." "In as much as you did it unto the least of these, you do it to Me."

For a moment we were quiet, with a longing to reach out to help them at Ground Zero.

I was reminded that the steeple fell but the church stands, a beacon of faith. So many around our table have had shattered dreams that we didn't know about, but perhaps drops of mercy came into blind eyes, or the oil of compassion for bruised hands and feet, and the balm of Gilead, God's love, for broken hearts.

It was just another ordinary Sunday dinner; or was it? When we take the cup and eat the bread and remember Him, God draws near in extraordinary ways.

Through the darkness of despair, hope slipped in to remind us that dawn was coming. Fear slithered out the back way while faith walked in the front doors into our hearts.

"Trust and Obey" — the only way.

Chapter Three

Bread Upon the Water

It was October 2001, soon after the day of infamy, September 11, when Ralph and I were on a plane to Boston. Jan would meet us in the baggage section to take us to the Gordon College Homecoming.

Ralph toured the campus he had attended years ago and saw the magnificent buildings and beautifully landscaped grounds; but more than that he realized that in a lovely, changing world, students are given a biblical world view.

Today, former students who entered the market place have become part of the solution to America's challenges, not a part of the problem as in earlier days of youthful indiscretions. Then they were boys! Today they are men! What they had been yesterday they were not today! I couldn't help but wonder if God would open a window and let Lena look into this day.

Lena, a symphony in black, with black flashing eyes and wisdom beyond her fifth-grade education, taught me how to pray with thanksgiving. For a moment I pictured myself back in the sixties as a college nurse. Lena, my cook and housekeeper, prayer partner and companion, was there when the restless youth had lost their moorings and drifted out to a sea of man's philosophy apart from godly principles. There was a blur of gray without the boundaries of black and white, right and wrong, good and evil. She could pierce that blur with her songs and stories, love and laughter, and somehow turn hearts away from distracting detours back to the main road.

Thirty years later, I still meet former students from Greensboro College who ask if Lena is still living. No one can forget her. She went Home in 1997, but left a legacy of child-like faith. How I miss her!

There was no gray with Lena; she was a fence to return to when someone was wandering in a pasture without fences. There was an air of authority as she walked tall, with her head held high.

When friends who didn't understand her sense of self esteem said, "Lena, you be so high and mighty," she would answer, "Why child, I be high and mighty, I be a child of the most high God. Can't get no higher."

When there was a problem, Lena said, "I best stretch out before the Lord," which meant to stretch out on a blanket on the floor and pray and wait for the answer. I had a tendency to figure out the answer, and then pray for God's approval.

"Stop organizing God," she would say to me; "Let God do it His way. If God could create the whole world, He can handle our problems."

She had a certain window in the kitchen from which to watch the students and "call out their name" (pray). When they came in, she usually had something to say.

"Lord have mercy, child, what are you doing with the skirt up to the 'possible?' Don't you know boys be looking for the 'possible' and you need to keep the 'possible' private? That's why we call some parts 'private.' Sit down, child, Lena needs to talk to you about the 'possible.'"

In the kitchen of the college infirmary, Lena held her own sex education classes; then between talks, she poured tea and sang songs.

One night, some students decided to jump the "rule fences" and had a party and some dared to streak naked across the campus in the darkness.

A photographer, hidden in the bushes, managed to get a

picture of one of our girls streaking across campus, no face visible. A maid across town overheard some elderly alumni, playing bridge, angrily hold up the newspaper picture and declare an end to their financial support.

"Such disgraceful behavior at a Methodist school."

The news came back to Lena, but she waited. She had her suspicions. One day her chance came when a girl stopped by for a glass of tea.

"Child, I heard tell that thousands of dollars going to be taken away from this school because you had to show your behind to the world; maybe some of that money helped your tuition."

"Lena, how did you know?"

"I took care of you when you were sick; I know that backside! Best thing you do now is make things right and ask forgiveness and keep your backside covered! Now sit down and have some tea."

On another day a student came in. "Now young man what's wrong with you? Look like you've been drove hard and put out wet."

"I'm getting kicked out of school."

"Not surprised! Been hearing about you partying with girls. Now I ask you, they going to pay your tuition? Besides that, what about all the pictures you got under your bed? You come from a big family, ten boys and girls, and I guess your mama dumped you all in the tub. Did you see anything new? God don't change the pattern. Girls be girls, boys be boys, same pattern!

"I heard tell your Papa and uncles work in a mill up North and you the first young-un to go to college. How your uncles and Papa gonna feel when you come home and have to work in the mill and waste all their money?"

"What should I do, Lena?"

"First off, cut that shaggy hair. You look like a rag doll. Get the fuzz off your face, put on a Sunday shirt, coat and tie, shine your shoes, then you go to the Dean man and you say:

'Mr. Dean man, I be so sorry and so ashamed. If you give me one more chance I will prove I can make it!' Now sit down and have some tea."

He graduated with honors. "Mr. Dean man" lives near me and we plan to have dinner and I'll tell him some stories he never knew, more than 30 years later.

· · · · · · ·

Gordon College was alive with former students returning to greet each other with, "Do you remember when?" They remembered!

Jan, the gracious hostess, planned a lovely dinner at the Wilson House, the president's home, and brought the former students together to share their journey from the sixties to the present.

It was a story of amazing grace!

Looking over the beautiful campus, I gazed at the peaceful lake that in the sixties was a scene of tragedy. It was a winter wonderland night when students in living color skated over the smooth ice.

The "rebels" on the far end of the lake, probably up to mischief, happened to see a student skate over the thin ice. Within moments they reached the scene, plunged in to grab the icy hand of their friend who had plunged into the frigid water.

They formed a chain while calling for help, but the hand slipped from the grasp, then was carried down stream out of sight.

Today they returned to look at the lake and remembered.

It was at this time that my son, Ralph, was in a far country, a long way from home and God, and the grief of knowing he was a lost sheep overwhelmed me with despair.

Lena, with her piercing black eyes looked at me and asked a question that turned a light on in my soul. "Who you be to tell God Almighty that He didn't do enough when He sent Jesus to die for your child, and now you think you have to die too? Jesus came that you might have life and your joy full. Praise is a detergent that cleans out the cobwebs of your mind so you can see God at work. You needs to unclog the channel; got the channel clogged up with bare feet and long hair, can't see God at work. Now, we sing the doxology and praise God from whom all blessings flow, even if you don't see the blessings; the believing comes before the seeing. Then we pray the promises of God, not the problems."

Nine months later, Ralph came home. It was September 15, 1970. Before long the hippies began to come to see what had happened to Ralph. Through the last of 1970 and through 1971 they came, about 70, and one weekend we had 19.

We took them in "as is;" God made them "as His."

Two came and lived with us for six months; one brought a baby raccoon that ate and slept with us, but when that raccoon used my shoe for a bathroom, I let out a scream!

They came shattered by their journey into the far country and through God's amazing grace the restoration began. During the restless nights, I sang lullabies, fed milk and crackers until the storm passed by. I didn't know the names of some of the hippies who found food and shelter from life's storms.

The Scripture says, "Cast thy bread upon the waters," (Ecclesiastes 11:1) but it seems to me we seldom see the return on earth.

They ate, slept, picked up the knapsack and left to wander, but prayer followed them and I somehow felt that there would be someone to lead the lost sheep home. Now, thirty years later, I, myself, was about to see the bread upon the waters return. It was October 5, 2001!

The main speaker was introduced as a Gordon graduate and an outstanding missionary in Mexico. He opened his Bible to Isaiah 66:1&2, "Thus saith the Lord. The heaven is my throne and the earth is my footstool: where is the house that ye build unto me? Where is the place of my rest?"

"For all those things hath my hand made, and all those things have been, saith the Lord, but to this man will I look, even to him that is poor and of a contrite spirit, and trembles at my word."

"Consider all that God has made yet what does he look for? A humble and a contrite heart, there He will abide!"

The speaker continued. "The church looks for a visitation but God looks for a habitation, a humble and a contrite heart. As God indwells us, the glory of the Lord will cover the earth as we reflect His presence."

I marveled how profound a simple message could be. I thought of the God of creation, living in a humble heart like Lena, and how His wisdom poured forth to bless and confound the wise of the world.

I watched the speaker with the open Bible and I saw a young man in cut-off jeans, bare feet in sandals, long hair and a beard, standing in my door with his brother, Keith, and the baby raccoon. I remembered the empty eyes, recalled the milk and crackers, the lullabies, more than 30 years ago. Now he stood before me, the main speaker, Kevin Grim!

Later, two handsome Gordon students stood before me. "We couldn't wait to meet you."

"Well, good looking, who are you?"

"We are Kevin's sons and want to thank you for taking our Dad into your home or we might not have been here. Thank you!"

"Cast thy bread upon the waters for thou shalt find it after many days."

I saw a blanket of blessings returning, or was it milk and crackers? I hear Lena singing, "Praise God from whom all blessings flow."

Chapter Four

Soup and Socks

With tears in my eyes, I braved a smile while I watched my grandson, Shawn, get behind the wheel of a Ryder truck, and with his Jeep in tow, turn down the road.

I didn't cry when his parents, Ralph and Chris, and brother, Eric, gathered around him to pray God's blessing and protection on the long journey before him. I just rubbed his shaved head and told him how proud I was of him and gave him mail to read when he was in a lonely motel room.

"I'm frightened," he admitted, "but also challenged, so I'm counting on your prayers." As I watched him disappear from view, I remembered the day I returned from a women's retreat and he met with me with a "Sit down, Grammy, I have something to tell you."

Before I left for the meeting he had asked me to pray about a decision he had to make and I agreed, thinking it had to do with a career opportunity after graduation from the University of North Carolina at Wilmington, so I prayed. Some outstanding opportunity must be waiting for this creative, talented grandson and finally someone has realized his potential, but...

"Grammy, I joined the Army!"

"Army?" Twenty-eight years old? Career? Family? But I stayed quiet and listened, then finally answered. "We prayed, and God does not trick us, so He will bless your decision."

"After September 11, I felt I had to go, I am single with no commitment to hold me back, so I'm on my way to Fort Knox, Kentucky, for basic training."

Ralph and Chris had attended his graduation from basic training and now he had emptied his belongings from my garage and filled the Ryder truck, and hooked up the Jeep.

Then he was gone! Then I cried!

After all there is a season for everything, and now alone, it was a good time for me to cry. Laugh and the world laughs with you, cry and you cry alone, came out of somewhere. I could hear my Norwegian Papa say, "*O ja,* so we are what we have been becoming." I wondered what this young man had been becoming.

When Shawn was around four years old, we had been building sandcastles one day on the shore of Wrightsville Beach when I told him to keep building his castle while I ran into the waves for a swim.

I swam a little but encountered a strong undertow and began struggling through the surf to the shore. Shawn looked up from his work of art and immediately ran into the water. "I'll help you, Grammy, I'll help you."

That was all I needed to hear. With sudden new power, I dashed for the shore where I grabbed my four-year-old hero and he yelled, "We did it! We did it!"

In one of his letters from Fort Knox he wrote, "We did it! We did it! A 28-mile hike. We did it!"

Now I could picture him heading out onto route I-40 and I wanted to call out to the world, "Watch out for that Ryder truck with the Jeep in tow. That's my grandson!"

· · · · · · ·

I brought my coffee cup into the den to watch the evening news.

Before me was displayed the power of the greatest military might on earth — airplanes, helicopters, giant tanks and well prepared troops. Knowing my grandson, Shawn, was part of that military power, I prayed for our leaders and especially for our troops. From a distance, I had seen bags of food flown in for the refugees and toys for the children, a gesture of friendship from our great country.

Suddenly I sat up, put my coffee cup down and watched soldiers from a world I knew little about, gather around a fire with our own military men to hold a cup of coffee on a cold winter day. I watched the group around the fire, holding soup or coffee, and saw warm socks given to the strange-looking soldiers. They couldn't speak English, but they understood the language of love through warm socks for cold feet. For a moment in time, a mystical people from a faraway land came into our hearts because of soup and socks which together brought the warmth of hope to a cold and lonely soul.

The picture of the faraway country brought me back to a four-room cottage, 500 square feet, in Saskatoon, Saskatchewan. Around the cottage, the Canadian wind whipped the falling snow into sculptured drifts. The frosted windowpanes made a convenient easel for young artists to display their creative talents.

When Saturday came, I pulled my sled beside Mama while we walked to the country store to get supplies for another week.

It was here she purchased the oatmeal which we sometimes ate three times a day, when the soup hit the bottom of the kettle, whole wheat flour for bread, butter and sugar lumps, coffee, apples with the brown spots, and the wilted vegetables at the week's end, and potatoes.

At the close of Mama's order, the owner gave Mama a bag of bones for soup. It was years later, after reading *First We have Coffee*, that the granddaughter of the owner of the store was told by her grandfather, "I remember that girl coming with her mother on Saturday, and I used to put extra meat with the bones because they fed many people. That never made headlines, but I have an idea that God has His Own 'Hall of Fame.'"

When I pulled the sled on our way home, our footsteps

crunching in the snow, Mama sang praises to God in Norwegian (Mama talked to God in Norwegian) and thanked Him for providing food for another week. What a sense of security for a ten-year-old girl to know that we had such a great God.

We were rich!

We hurried our steps, but I wished these walks could last longer, because it was then, when we were alone, when Papa was away on a long missionary journey, that she could share some of her heart. She talked to me like an adult, and it took years for me to realize that the stories and truths I learned from her came from those walks to the country store. I also began to understand how lonely she must have been at times.

It was warm in the kitchen. Mama sang, "Count your blessings one by one" as she unloaded the groceries for the week. Life was good!

· · · · · · ·

When I watched our men giving socks to the other solders, I couldn't help but remember Mama and a cold winter day.

"Mama, Mr. Hansen is here again!"

"*O ja*, tell him to come in and sit by the stove."

Mr. Hansen was a burly-looking Norwegian with red hair and a beard.

"Sit, sit, Mr. Hansen, a cup of coffee and a bowl of soup will do you good."

This was a nightly ritual. He never laughed or told stories like Uncle Barney, just sat staring into space.

"Mama, what's the matter with Mr. Hansen?"

"*O ja*, he has a sickness of the soul; his Hilda won't come from Norway. She is afraid to cross the ocean and leave her home, so he waits, sick from loneliness of the soul."

"But, Mama, his feet smell so bad."

"*Ja*, I know. I will think of something. Sometimes it is hard for men to be alone, especially Norwegian men who have had mama, grandma, aunts and sisters to spoil them."

The following night, when Mr. Hansen arrived, Mama said,

"Now, Mr. Hansen, it is so cold outside; take off your shoes and socks and soak your feet in this tub of hot water."

With a wink at me, Mama put drops of Lysol in the water!

"*O ja*, that is good."

He sat with his feet in the Lysol water while Mama took his socks, stiff enough to stand, washed and hung them up behind the cook stove to dry. Quietly he ate the bowl of soup, and drank the coffee with a sugar lump.

"Now, Mr. Hansen, just put on Papa's socks and your feet will feel much better."

Night after night Mr. Hansen came to soak his feet in Lysol water while Mama washed his socks and fed him soup.

One night, he came bursting with joy.

"My Hilda, she comes, oh, my Hilda, she comes."

That ended the foot washing ceremony in the kitchen. More than 75 years have passed, yet I saw again how hope can rise up on wings of soup and socks.

Chapter Five

Above the Clouds

One day I stood in the Providence, Rhode Island airport with three bags, unable to move since the lines were endless. I wasn't sure if I was in front or back, so I just stood still! I needed to get to Baltimore, where I could catch a flight to Greensboro, North Carolina.

After endless calls to my faithful travel agent, Rhonda, I had taken her advice, "Just go, and take a chance, even if you have to spend the night in the airport. Everything is closed, so try to get to Providence."

Chad, my No.1 Grandson, had broken the speed records to get me there.

"Don't move, Grammy, I'll be right back."

I couldn't move! Within moments I heard, "Chad Carlberg," paged over the speaker. He returned the page, and then came to me with a charming smile, "No problem." That is usually when I worry.

I heard, "Yes, sir, I will take good care of her," and I was ushered into first class with a big hug. "Gotta go. See, I told you, no problem." He raced off to make an appointment for a critical interview about his film, a documentary on baseball in the Dominican Republic.

When I boarded the plane, I looked into the cockpit to tell the pilot that the first thing I do on boarding is to pray for the pilot, crew and passengers.

"I want you to know I am praying for you today, for God's protection over you and the plane."

"Oh, thank you. My wife is praying too," he added.

With tears in her eyes the stewardess reached out to me, "Thank you, thank you." For a moment I held a frightened "heroine." She was there in spite of her fears following 9/11, and I whispered, "You'll make it."

Other passengers came on board and they smiled and nodded as though to say, "We are all in this together and we need each other."

While waiting for clearance, I had time to be quiet and review the events of the past days.

• • • • • • •

After the chapel service, one that would remain in our hearts for always, Dr. Carlberg announced that the chapel would remain open, with faculty and staff available to pray with students.

I watched Dr. Nelson place a fatherly arm around Jud Carlberg and pray for God's guidance, protection and wisdom in the days ahead.

"We often forget how leaders give so much of themselves, we need to pray for them," Eldred Nelson added.

With tears in her eyes, Jan held frightened students in her arms to pray for them. Young people, who hadn't faced the hurricanes of life, now realized their future would be forever changed.

Upon our return to the Wilson House, Jan put a roast in the oven.

It reminded me of a long ago time when crisis faced our family and my Norwegian Mama quietly put on the coffee pot.

When faced with situations over which we have no control, it is wise to reach out and do what we can control. A "spot of tea" in the midst of heartbreak can help us to take a deep breath and to take the next step.

Mama's "First we have coffee" preached the tackling of problems. "Faith and works go together. *O ja*, you just do what you have to do, what is in your hand; then faith takes you the rest of the way." (I wonder if *Bestemor* is watching her granddaughter, Jan, as she delegates duties to everyone around her?)

Within moments we found aprons and put our hands to work while we placed the pain in our hearts on "hold." Ruth Nelson peeled potatoes, Rut, from Norway, cut up fruit for a salad, and I found a stool at the bar to sit on with a bowl of apples to peel and slice for Jan's famous apple crisp.

The men kept up a lively conversation, moved chairs in place, then greeted the children as they came out of the storm and into a safe place, home.

Heather and husband, Matt, came with two-year-old Lily for a break from hospital duties as medical residents under the Harvard program at Cambridge.

Chad came with his friends, "Smells like Sunday dinner at Grammy's."

The aproned cooks, the aroma of home, the warm greetings of love brought a whisper of hope to the unasked question, "How, now, shall we live?"

Chuck Colson never dreamed when he wrote his great book that it could be part of the process to prepare a terrorized people for the "now" of living. There are times when the ordinary becomes extraordinary in the adversity of human events.

With all the family and guests joining hands around the table, I recalled a message given at chapel some years ago when the speaker said, "When we gather around a table it is like commemorating the Eucharist when Jesus said, 'Take, eat! Remember me.'" The blessing that Jud Carlberg offered at the table was remembering the family, the nation, but it was also remembering Him.

We ate, and after leisurely drinking a cup of coffee, we helped to bring order to the kitchen.

Beautiful music came from the grand piano while Ruth's

fingers rolled over the keys to bring the old hymns of faith to feed the soul.

"Come, Matt," Eldred Nelson called, "We need your tenor voice."

Matt and Heather curled up in a big arm chair, while Lily found a "safe place" in a secure lap.

It was the sound of faith above the storm.

I was brought back to the present.

. . . .

The plane was off the ground, flying high above the clouds in a peaceful world over the tragedy below.

I remembered how Harold, my husband of 53 years, used to say, "A crisis doesn't make a man, but reveals who he is."

How do you prepare for the tragedies of life?

"The process is the plan," says Corrie Ten Boom.

My Norwegian Papa used to say, "*O ja*, we are what we have been becoming."

When I get home, I'll review my journal from the past years and see what this family has been becoming.

Finally the plane landed in Baltimore and I was able to catch a plane to Greensboro. I would be met and taken to the historic Fort Caswell by the sea, where I was due to speak at a women's retreat.

My angel Chris, Ralph's wife, had filled in for me on Friday night and conducted a beautiful candlelight service. Now I was expected to continue the service on Saturday.

I was on my way!

We arrived at Fort Caswell, North Carolina, at 2:00 a.m. and a guard opened the gate to let us through. A soft wind blew over from the ocean and we could hear the sound of rolling surf.

With open arms, Chris was there to tuck me into bed, then promised to awaken me at 8:00 a.m. with coffee and donuts. She did!

With a warm welcome, I was ushered into a room filled

with beautiful women whose upturned faces reflected the unspoken question that Chuck Colson used to title his book, *How Now Shall We Live?*

As I recalled the events that I had encountered, I saw hope slip up through the cracks of unbelief, like a blade of grass that creeps up through the concrete in my driveway.

The women could see with eyes of faith, 1,500 Gordon students and friends singing "Great is Thy Faithfulness," and somehow faith rose up slowly to tread softly into a new era.

I continued. "When I stood in that crowded Providence airport, suddenly out of nowhere, an operatic tenor sang, 'Oh say, does that star spangled banner yet wave o'er the land of the free and the home of the brave?'"

An awesome hush descended over the airport, as in silence we stood with a hand over the heart; faces turned toward the unseen soloist. When he hit the high note, "land of the free and the home of the brave," the airport erupted in tumultuous applause, not only for the soloist, but for America, the land of the free, and the home of the brave.

"No terrorist can touch the soul of America."

For a moment there was silence in the conference room; then we stood to hold hands to pray for our President Bush, our leaders, our nation and the empty hearts and homes of suffering people.

We prayed for ourselves that we would be light and salt to a world with broken dreams.

It was time for a break before the next session.

I stopped for a cup of coffee and to autograph books. A beautiful young lady came to me, saying, "My world is crashing around me, I feel shattered, only despair."

For a moment I thought of crashing towers, toppled steeple, and I realized once more there are many unseen terrorists of fear, hate, unforgiveness, despair and guilt that comes crashing against the purposes of God in a life.

Quietly, I shared the greatest story ever told, that God so loved the world that He gave His son, that if she believed in

Him, in this Jesus, the life, the truth, the way, she would have eternal life and belong to God for always. She could be set free from the shackles that were shattering her life and she would find grace for each new day.

Faith came on slippered feet to topple her tower of fear: hope came through the cracks of unbelief: but it was love that drew her to the Father's heart, through a child-like faith in Jesus, His Son.

> *Mercy there was great and grace was free,*
> *Pardon there was multiplied for me,*
> *there my burdened heart found liberty,*
> *at Calvary.*

— Hymn: Calvary-Newell-Towner,
The New Church Hymnal, page 438

Softly she whispered, "I believe."
Love rose up where her towers had fallen.

· · · · · · ·

My journey had come to an end, and I was safely home, curled up with my down pillow and comforter. "Oh God, forsake me not until I have shown Thy strength to this generation and Thy power to everyone to come." (Isaiah 71:18)

The grandfather clock chimed midnight! A new day was on the way.

Chapter Six

A Memorable Retreat
===================

"Since I am flying into Chicago on United, Mom, I'll meet you at the US Air gate. Then we can proceed to the United gate for Traverse City, Michigan. From there we rent a car to drive to Mackinaw City and take a ferry to Mackinaw Island."

When I hung up the phone, I chuckled to myself.

"That's my organized daughter. Jan will have every hour planned and all I have to do is follow the instructions. Now I have a list for my granddaughter Kathryn Elise: take care of the mail, keep my faithful Doberman happy — and get me to the airport on time.

It was October 2001, when we made our way through security to the ticket counter where my friendly US Air agent, Steve, greeted me: "Here she comes, on the road again and I see you are on your way to the windy city. Mighty brave to travel after September 11th."

"I'm thankful to see your familiar face and I just keep praying for safety for us all, and by the way, the safest place is to be in God's will."

A ticket and a hug and I'm on my way to Chicago. Lines were everywhere in Chicago, a far cry from the familiar hometown airport. As I passed through security, my number came up and I was searched and I mean searched, all my bags and off with my shoes! I was concerned that our connection to Traverse

City would be missed.

There is something comforting about a small-town airport where you are known by your name, not just a number.

I thought about a story my friend Mary told me when she monitored the halls in high school. She made it a point to know the names of "could be" troublemakers so she called out their names, "Hi Joe, how're things going?" One day a shy young girl slipped up to Mary and said, "If I tell you my name would you call it out? I just want someone to know me."

Here I was, just a number, with someone going through my underwear while I stood shoeless.

Out of the maze of strangers a big black man with a million-dollar smile came with a wheel chair.

"So your number came up," he chuckled. "I know the back way and I'll race this chariot and you'll make your connection."

In all the confusion of emptying everything I owned, I lost my driver's license.

"Take your seat," he said, "Nothing's lost, just slipped into a pocket."

"Praise the Lord," I exclaimed. "Sure enough, it slipped into a pocket."

"I knew you'd find it," my new friend added, "we just need each other and we need the Lord. Hard times right now, but God won't fail."

"God bless you, Sam," and we were quickly on our way to make our connection at the United gate, but with a deeper awareness that Sam and I were family, part of the family of God and He knew our names!

When Jan and I arrived in Traverse City, a lovely room was ready, with soft beds, down pillows and comforters.

"What a luxury, Jan, usually the pillows are as hard as the beds but this is wonderful!"

"I'm not surprised that your number came up, all that beeping with your hair pins and clips, but I think the Canadian passport is following you — a marked woman! Oh, if I could only stop you from telling a story to everyone you meet! What am I going to do with you, Mother?"

"You'll have to admit that life is never boring when we hit the road."

While we unpacked our suitcases I remembered the passport story.

· · · · · · ·

It was another October 1995, when Jan and I were invited to have a book table at Hoste Fest, a Norwegian festival held at the fairgrounds at Minot, North Dakota. We were at the airport when a plane filled with Norwegians from Norway landed and they stepped off the plane wearing colorful Norwegian sweaters and waving Norwegian flags, laughing and talking at the same time. About 100,000 visitors come from all over to celebrate the annual Norwegian festival.

Our book table was in a corner but we also had the opportunity to attend the dramatic shows and visit the endless booths displaying creative talent.

One morning when we were setting up our books, Jan said, "Look, Mom, the Norwegian bachelors, from Garrison Keillor's Lake Woebegone are coming."

I looked up and saw two handsome men, about 6' 6" tall, blonde, blue eyed, and wearing identical Norwegian sweaters.

"We are twins," they said, "farmers from Minnesota. Come, we want to show you what we bought for the farmhouse."

They led us to a booth where an artist was displaying her rosemalling art on a clock.

"That is the one we bought."

The artist laughed, "That's not all they bought; in fact that farm house is filled with my art work."

We watched her while she brushed her scroll like art of brilliant colors on chests, furniture and small items. It is beautiful Norwegian art with definite design and color. I have a small plaque in my breakfast room: Velkommen (welcome) in rosemalling art.

The way the "bachelors" looked at her, I had a sneaking

feeling they were both in love with her — just a hunch.

"*Ja*, that we have. Mama and Papa are gone, but we keep the house just like Mama did. *Ja*, so now perhaps we go get a cup of coffee and *lefse*."

The abundance of food was everywhere and we were told that the Lutheran church brought in the *Lute Fisk*, a slippery fish with melted butter, and it seemed to me that slippery fish came in tons! (We used to beg for meatballs, but mama thought we were a disgrace to Norway not to eat the special Christmas delicacy.)

Now *lefse*, that is different! In Decorah, Iowa, the Penny Department Store emptied out their front windows so the women, in Norwegian dress, could make *lefse* for the world to watch. They rolled out the dough (very thin) and baked it on special irons, then rolled it up with butter, sugar & cinnamon. The lines reached out a block to get this delicacy. So much for just a little *lefse*!

After a friendly visit, our coffee and *lefse*, we went back to our book table to visit with people from all over the country; many were from Canada who had seen us on "100 Huntley Street," a Toronto T.V. program.

A man came over to look at Jan's devotional book, *The Hungry Heart*, and asked, "What has this to do with Scandinavian culture?"

Jan's beautiful smile and quiet reply, "The Carlberg name," brought a chuckle.

One young man came over to us and said, "I'm from California, not even Norwegian, but I come each year because it is like the family I don't have; probably the friendliest, most joyful people who treasure their heritage, yet deeply patriotic toward America. I just want to feel a part of it."

"You know Jan, I think celebrations are like fences to come back to, a stirring up of joy, almost like banking blessings for the lonesome days."

I wondered for a moment if the weary travelers of the world come to the overflowing bank of joy in our community of

Christ followers, or is our bank of joy overdrawn?

After a week at *Hoste Fest*, we were ready to pack up and head across the border to Birch Hills, Saskatchewan, in a red, rented sports car.

At the border we were asked for our identification and, in my enthusiasm, I rattled off about how excited I was to return to the place where my father pitched the tent in the summertime and as a preacher held services in the schoolhouse during the winter months.

"I love Canada, and many of my stories come from my Canadian childhood. (I didn't get Jan's nudge in time.) *First We Have Coffee* is about my immigrant parents and I'd like to autograph a book for you."

When I stopped long enough for a breath I looked into a hard face, with cold steely eyes. "Come inside! You need to fill our work papers!"

"Work papers! I just tell stories!"

"Do you get paid?"

"I hope so." (Big mistake.) "I went with my father when he pitched the tent." (Jan's knee reached me and I stopped!)

After about 30 minutes she let us go, clearly not interested in my book or Papa's tent meetings.

"Mom, next time just say you are visiting friends and leave Grandpa's tent out of the picture. That woman took the book offer as a bribe! We're lucky to be on the road again."

Before we left Minot, we had been encouraged to keep emergency supplies in our car. "You never know when a winter blizzard sweeps across the prairie. Flashlight, extra blanket, and chocolate bars."

Enough was enough, so I decided to take a nap, no more stories on this trip. (No blizzard, but we ate the candy bars.)

Upon our arrival in Birch Hills, we were welcomed with love and good old Scandinavian hospitality. Of course they thought the story was hilarious, but I found out it wasn't that humorous.

On a later flight to Canada, when I was a speaker at the

Prairie Bible Institute's 70th anniversary services, I waited in line.

"Please tell the people I'm right here so they don't think I missed the plane."

"Stay in line!"

I stayed!

When I looked around, I noticed I was in the line with some strange looking people, long hair, beads and chains; there I stood, an innocent looking grandmother with white hair. Finally, I was called inside and made the comment that I often traveled to Canada and why was I stopped now?

"Silence!"

Suddenly the young woman at the desk burst out laughing. I didn't see anything that humorous.

"Someone marked your passport 'Criminally inadmissible.' (That was funny?) By the way, what do you do?"

"I'm a storyteller." I wasn't about to tell her about Papa's tent.

"Well, it looks like you have another story," then waved me on. (I wasn't about to offer her a book either.)

That was another day, and now I am back to the present — unpacking.

. . . .

"Perhaps we ought to do a book, Jan. 'Have suitcase, will travel.' We have some good travel stories of getting lost, sleeping in airports, and riding with strange men, especially fast moving taxi cab drivers."

After a good night's sleep, we were ready to say a reluctant goodbye to down pillows and Traverse City, and begin our delightful trek in a rented car along Lake Michigan toward Mackinaw City, then take a ferry to Mackinaw Island.

Along the way, we passed a number of cherry orchards and realized we were in the cherry capital of the world. Then we passed a farm with pumpkins hanging from the trees. (Why is my camera packed when I need it?)

We could have spent a week in Mackinaw City, with their

stories of wrecked ships and lives lost on the great Lakes, tales of lighthouses, drama and music, and a visit to Fort Mackinaw which the British constructed during the American Revolution. We couldn't tarry because we were booked for a certain departure time on the Arnold Ferry. This ferry has served the public since 1878, and when it took us to Mackinaw Island, we stepped back in time to horse-drawn carriages.

The Grand Hotel there defies description in its majestic Victorian splendor. Attendants in colorful uniforms escorted us to the Governor's Suite, where we wandered around in spacious rooms, knowing our time is limited in that impressive setting, since we are scheduled for two, back to back retreats and since accommodations are limited to 1000 people at each retreat.

Five-course meals were served us by handsome waiters from Jamaica, running rhythm while balancing large platters of food. At night the waiters held their own Gospel service in the Catholic Church, where the joy of the Lord kept visitors singing past midnight.

In the midst of all the creative beauty surrounding us, the vivid colors of coral and green, profusion of geraniums, soft carpets and beautiful rooms with portraits of our first ladies, the women came, some with empty souls, broken hearts, fearing the terror that threatened America. They came to a mending basket called "Winsome Women's Retreat."

No one cancelled because of September 11th. They knew there was a fence to return to, a place where they could be renewed in faith, refreshed in sprit, encouraged by stories of faith and strengthened by God's word. They came to stand together in prayer for our nation and seek God's help in this time of need.

Just as God's love reached into a stable in Bethlehem and invaded history with a baby's cry, so God, by His Holy Spirit, flowed through the setting of creative beauty and reached into the empty places. Like the thread in Mama's mending basket that filled the hole in the socks, God's love moved through crevices of doubt, brokenness and emptiness with the thread of hope.

It just takes a measure of faith to reach up and receive grace and mercy at Calvary. Soon it was time to leave, as horse-drawn carriages stood in line to take us to the ferry.

In the midst of all the goodbyes, Jan mentioned passing the farm with the pumpkins.

"That's my farm," a woman called out. "My husband tied those pumpkins on the trees with baling wire after someone asked, 'How do pumpkins grow.' Jokingly someone answered, 'on trees,' so he decided to tie the pumpkins on trees. Now it has become a tourist attraction. Please stop by our farm on your drive back to Traverse City."

We did!

When we pulled up to the farm we saw a family making donuts, putting up cherry jam, baking pies, and making plans for a community celebration with a hot dog roast and country music.

Munching on a hot donut we looked around and asked, "What can we do for you?"

The father gathered his family and asked, "Would you pray for us?"

We formed a circle and Jan prayed God's blessing on the family and the farm with the hanging pumpkins.

Goodbyes and hugs go together; then we were on our way to Traverse City. This farm woman had just been a part of the beautiful setting of the Grand Hotel; now she was back in blue jeans and plaid shirts, putting her hands and feet to the task. Her soul had been refreshed, her faith restored and her hope rekindled for the new dawn.

When we returned to our comfort zone, we packed our bags for our return flight to Chicago; then Jan would go to Boston and I would fly south.

I remembered that when we had spoken at the Grand Hotel some time ago, I had the Betty Ford room, in soft mint green, and Jan had the Roselyn Carter room done in Georgia peach.

When Jan answered the phone, one of the retreat leaders said she would be right up with the morning schedule. We proceeded to empty our suitcases and put on nightgowns. I had brushed back my hair in a ponytail — then the knock at the door.

"Come on in!"

There stood a guide leading a tour group to see the "First Lady" rooms and their lovely portraits. They got more than they bargained for and the laughter echoed down the hall.

One of the musicians was missing from the final banquet and I whispered, "What happened?"

"He couldn't take any more five course meals so he headed out for a one course meal, a hamburger!"

There are times when blessings can overtake us and our cup runs over; then God allows a "dry spell," a hamburger instead of a banquet.

Our journey had come to an end and I was home, under my own down comforter. At midnight, the grandfather clock chimed out the hoof beats of hope that slipped in before the down, a reminder that our times are in God's Hands.

For everything — a season
That goes beyond our reason.
A time for tears to wash our eyes
To see God, who hears our cries.
A time to sing, to laugh, to play
A time to wait at close of day.
A time to sit at setting sun
Toiling is over, race well run.
A time to stand for what is right
Unflinching trust in Godly might.
A time to look beyond earth's maze
And see God's love, amazing grace.

— M. T. J.

Chapter Seven

The Mending Basket

It was good to return home on a pleasant flight from Little Rock, Arkansas, to the familiar faces at the Wilmington Airport. There was Kathryn Elise, my youngest granddaughter, to retrieve my bags from the conveyer belt and head for the familiar road to home!

"Did you have a good time with Aunt Joyce and all the cousins?" "It was a special Thanksgiving in your Aunt Judy's beautiful new home; and yes, all the aunts, uncles and cousins. We talk about Papa and Uncle Howard as though they were right there; but that's what memories do, keep our loved ones near."

On Saturday morning, my sister, Joyce, and I took off to an antique store in Russellville, called Collectors Gallery. We could spend a week there going from aisle to aisle to see memories of another day. Now Aunt Joyce can find treasures, and I seem to miss them, but I keep looking for, now don't laugh, a wooden egg."

"A wooden egg?"

"Under this sink I have a bag of your brother's 'holey' basketball socks that I use for cleaning rags. Believe me, my Mama would have no such thing. Those socks would go in a mending basket where she kept a smooth round wooden egg to slip in to the toes or heels, then mend with yarn until sometimes there was more mending than sock. There was magic in that basket where it seemed that God and Mama could repair anything from socks to souls."

"When I was in nurse's training, I had to wear black cotton stockings. Then I was given a gift of silk hose, a treasure that I mended carefully with silk thread. These stockings had a seam in the back and we had to keep it straight or be considered 'tacky.'"

"Thank goodness for pantyhose! I'll put the tea kettle on, Grammy, while you unpack and finish the story about the mending basket."

"I remember when you were about three years old, and I rocked you and told you stories about my childhood. You looked up and said, 'I'd like to go to heaven so *Bestemor* can tell me stories and sing songs like she did for you.'"

"Do you remember everything I said?"

"Oh yes, I write it down, and then I can tell my children what you used to do. There is nothing like a grilled cheese and a cup of tea after airplane pretzels and cokes."

"What about the mending basket?"

· · · · · · ·

The mending basket sat next to a small rocker in the parlor, and that basket held anything that needed mending.

One day, when I was about ten years old, I happened to look out the window and I called, "Mama, I think Mrs. Olsen is coming and it looks like she is crying."

"*O ja*, Margaret, you answer the door if she comes here, and I will put on the coffee pot." Within minutes, Mama had taken off her "work apron," and put on a white starched "company apron" that she kept on a nail in the kitchen, in case somebody comes."

With her soft brown hair brushed back, she greeted her visitor with a cheerful, "Oh, how good to see you Mrs. Olsen, and to think I just put on the coffee pot, so nice to have someone for afternoon coffee." No matter how busy Mama was she just reached for the "company apron" and had a warm greeting for everyone.

You see I knew how busy my Mama was, always working, cooking, scrubbing clothes on a washboard, baking all the bread, and that's not all. She made all our clothes out of the missionary barrel. I could hear the treadle machine at night, such a good sound to think God and Mama never slept. She kept a spotless house. I know, because she taught me how to scrub, and she even had starched curtains in the outhouse — oh well, you don't even know what an "outhouse" is.

I watched the younger children. (To think we were five children in that tiny 500 square feet cottage, with no running water. By the way, your Aunt Joyce was born in that house.) I heard Mama say, "Come, come, Mrs. Olsen, sit down, sit down. I baked bread yesterday so we have bread and sugar lumps." They always called each other Mrs. or Mr.; Mama called Papa "Mr. Tweten" to others when talking about him. It was a mark of civility and respect.

Mama pretended not to see anything wrong and poured coffee and began a story, something she knew how to do.

> "Oh you can't imagine what Mr. Tweten did one day. When he rides the bicycle, he rolls up the trouser leg and fastens the pant legs with a clip, so the trousers don't get caught in the spokes or get dirty.
>
> "So, Mr. Tweten goes off and the next thing I know he is on the platform with these rolled up trousers, so I wrote a note for the usher, and Mr. Tweten picked up the note and reads it out loud, 'Papa please take down your pants.'
>
> "You should have heard them laughing so hard," Mama wiped her eyes with her apron.

She poured another cup of coffee; this was for the sugar lump; then Mrs. Olsen said, "I must go home now and put on the potatoes. Norwegian women always "put on the potatoes," even if they don't know what else to serve — but always potatoes.

Mrs. Olsen left, still laughing, headed down the path and I

asked, "Mama, why didn't you ask her why she was crying?"

"Oh, Margaret, sometimes a cup of coffee is enough, not always so good to tell everything; also time is a great healer."

"What did my grandmother look like?"

"To me she was the most beautiful woman in the world, and Papa said that all the time. I thought she was so tall, but she was only about 5 feet 4 inches, slender, even after seven children.

"My Papa was like a rushing waterfall; but Mama was like a quiet river. She had soft brown hair and she would let me brush her beautiful hair and then she would twist it into a figure eight. She used to buy Raleigh shampoo and some kind of ointment that we used for everything. It came in a round, blue container.

"Now, my Papa had a high forehead, blonde hair swept back and beautiful sky-blue eyes that took in the world; but Mama's blue-grey eyes looked at you with her penetrating gaze and at night she would say, 'Margaret, is there anything you need to tell me before we talk to God?'"

"What did you do?"

"I just rattled off anything I could remember, like if I tattled on Grace, or didn't watch my brother. Once I told her how sorry I was that I emptied the chamber pot in the cook stove and put the fire out."

"You did what?"

"Well, it was so cold that I didn't want to carry the pot to the outhouse. (Mama said chamber was a better word than pot.) Papa was furious. The fire was out but the odor stayed."

"Oh, Grammy, I can't believe you did that. Did you tell a lie or steal something?"

"Oh, heavens no, but I did listen at the key hole, especially if Papa had a wedding in the parlor. I wanted to see them kiss."

"Those were small things."

"Mama said there were no small sins, just sin."

"What did she do?"

"Quietly she said, '*Ja*, that is good to tell everything before you go to bed; then we ask God's forgiveness.' My Mama was very strict, but loving and patient and we adored her, but Papa had a temper. No one answered our parents back, even if we "thought" rebellion, we had deep love and respect for them. It was wonderful to have Mama tuck us in, knowing we were squared away with God and Mama."

"Let's get back to the mending basket, Grammy."

· · · · · · ·

"One evening Mrs. Peterson came, and Mama told me to take care of the children and get them ready for bed and not to listen."

"Since I was the eldest, she often confided in me. 'Sometimes people need more than a cup of coffee, they need the precious gift of time.' I understood.

Mama settled her guest in the parlor; then took her place in the rocker where her mending basket sat. The troubled guest poured out her soul, while Mama nodded and quietly reached into the basket for the wooden egg, her fingers flew with the woolen yarn while one then another sock was mended. Mama nodded, listened, added a word here and there; then reached for my rag doll, torn and tattered, but Mama knew how much that doll mattered, so the stitches showed that the mending was thorough."

"Oh, thank you, Mrs. Tweten, you have helped me so much. Now, I know I can face tomorrow."

"Now, it is time for a cup of coffee and a sugar lump; then we must turn the burden over to the Lord and leave it there."

"I peeked. Mama hugged Mrs. Peterson, then she was gone."

"Mama, you didn't say anything."

"Oh, so you listened?"

"Not really, I just heard her talking and talking but you

were so quiet. So what did you do to help her?"

Mama took my face between her hands and said softly, "Look, my mending basket is empty. Someday you will learn that hearts need mending like stockings."

I happened to go through some old papers the other day and found this one I wrote thirty-five years ago, all wrinkled and faded but I'll sit here at the foot of the bed and read it to you.

The Mending Basket

The basket stood by the old rocking chair,
full of socks and tatters in need of repair,
And the day sped by: night shadows came.
The basket filled up again and again.
Oh, tomorrow, a day with time to spare
I'll get to the mending, a wishful prayer...
The toes came through and the heels wore thin
and Mama tried again to begin.
The children called, a doorbell rang,
the bread was baking, teakettle sang.
Soup needed stirring, and Papa a shirt;
There was cooking, baking, feeding our crew,
the endless guests came for Mama's stew.
Then late one night another came,
with a broken life and heart of pain,
Mama sat in the old rocking chair,
listening to burdens with a quiet prayer,
reached into the basket, found a sock,
slipped in the darning egg, smooth as a rock.
The fingers moved gently and covered a hole
while a heart, bruised and broken poured out her soul.
Again the darning egg slipped into place.
Heals and toes mended, tatters replaced.
Mama's fingers moved yarn to and fro,

While the heart listened to tales of woe,
The darning egg slipped from toe to heel,
One pair, then ten, Mama could feel
The basket was empty, time to stop,
Bread was warm, and a fresh coffee pot
Perked on the stove and filled the room,
Hearts were lifted from despair and gloom.
For Mama had listened and quietly prayed
While the darning egg slipped through stockings frayed
And the heart, heavy burdened released its load.
Some reach for the stars and climb mountain tops,
But God comes down while mending socks
To fill the hole in the soul with His loving Hand
And mends with His grace the life He planned.

— M.T.J., 1969

"Goodnight my Katrinka (nickname), sleep well."

"I love you, Grammy."

Quietly, I checked on the dog, curled up on her pillow, turned off the lights and slipped under my down comforter. It had been a long journey to the little house in Canada and the mending basket. Tomorrow I'll come back to the present. Maybe I'll find that wooden egg.

Chapter Eight

Betrayal and Forgiveness

"Sit down! I have something to tell you."

I held the phone in my hand with a premonition that this conversation was not one I wanted to hear, but I sat down.

"I have been betrayed! My John (not the true name) has had a mistress for several years. Oh, I loved him so much. He was a good father, a leader in the church and community, successful and respected in business, and my best friend. He was always so dependable, my anchor, to think he made love to me, and oh (she sobbed), to think he went to other arms when he said that he had to work late."

"I thought he was a workaholic and begged him to take care of himself. How can he not see how he is destroying the lives of his family! Divorce! I never dreamed such a thing could happen to us."

For a moment I thought about Mama's mending basket and how she kept the yarn moving over the hole in the sock, while God reached down to mend the hole in the soul. I remembered again what Mama said to me, "I listened."

Now I sat in stunned silence listening and grasping for a word of profound wisdom, some comfort to offer.

I heard a beautiful child of God, loving, giving, trusting, but now the words came hurling across the airwaves, bitter, shocking, frightened and angry words that hit the airwaves like hail on a tin roof.

Then came an exhausted pause. Quietly I asked, "Who is there to help you?"

"My family and they're so wonderful, and I have a good lawyer," (practical, I thought) "and my pastor and church family. Oh, how do you go on when life that was filled with dreams comes to a dead end?"

"My dear Jane, for someone so young you have shown great wisdom in your choice of counselors and you have more courage and strength than you realize. Would you like a prayer?"

"Oh, yes, please!"

"Oh, loving Father, hold this precious child in Your arms of love and lavish her with the wisdom, guidance and understanding she needs to take one step at the time. Amen."

"I'm proud of you for being the loving, faithful wife and devoted mother. You have been, and for such a time as this, I am confident you will make the right decisions." I put down the phone and pondered the many truths I longed to share, but there would be another time when the mind and heart could listen.

I remembered a day in the long ago when I had been betrayed, and in my grief dared anyone to throw scripture verses at me. They would feel like hailstones. I longed to hear, "You are loved." Then came a merciful moment when a white-haired servant of God took me in his arms and said "I love you, and God loves you. You are safe in the hollow of His hand." The whisper of hope slipped through the cracks of my tattered soul. I learned that forgiveness brings healing.

I sat down and wrote a letter to John, the one who had betrayed his family. I begged him to return to the fork of the road where the deception began and then turn his heart and life back to his family. Love and forgiveness, with a truly repentant spirit can restore the broken years and lives can be repaired.

When John rejected the road to the cross, the pivot upon which time turns, the cross that towers over the wrecks of time, the place where grace and mercy meet, I knew he would face the dark night of the soul.

The Cross

I saw your hand outstretched for me,
I saw your love from Calvary,
I looked, and then I turned away.
I wanted oh so much to live,
I thought the world had it all to give;
I looked again, this time I walked away.
I never knew that I could cry so many tears;
I never knew that I'd be counting wasted years;
I'm coming back to You.
My lonely days and nights are through;
I'm turning around to see
those outstretched arms for me.
I'm coming home, I'm coming home
I'm so tired of trying to make it on my own.
I'm coming back to you,
my lonely days and nights are through.
I'm turning around to see
those outstretched arms for me.

— M.T.J.

I knew the safe place for John was back at the cross that leads home. I prayed for Jane to grow strong and to have the "stretching out" kind of faith that stands tall in the storm. Another time we could talk about forgiveness, not being an option, but an act of the will. When you pray, forgive! In the meantime, the cruelty of betrayal would grow less sharp and the listening heart could hear.

After I had done what I could, I knew I had to release the burden to the "burden bearer" and pack my suitcase for the next trip to the airport.

Within a few hours I was in another hotel room, unpacking my bags and getting ready for the morning session. I had just come from another retreat where 80% of the women had been raped or abused, and I was still in shock.

Later in the day a beautiful woman came to me. "I need to talk to you about my friend."

We found a quiet corner.

"My friend was gang raped, and she lost count when she passed out."

Having grown up in my safe place, with my Norwegian Mama who walked softly with God, and my Papa, who had a stand-up kind of faith, I realized again that they were my fences of protection from the evil around us. My Sunday school theme song had been, "I would be true for there are those who trust me."

Suddenly the woman in front of me trembled, "How can I ever forget?" She cried through clenched fists. "Oh, I'm sorry, I didn't mean to give myself away."

As I reached for her, she cried out, "I guess if I had a shotgun, I'd be tempted to mow them down, such unbelievable horror."

"My dear, there is a better way!"

"What's better?"

"Forgiveness is better."

"Forgiveness?"

"Yes, forgiveness takes the evil out of our clutching hands, straining for revenge, and puts it into God's hands, and He says 'Vengeance is mine.' God's justice against evil will outstrip our imagination. Jesus says for us to pray, 'Forgive us, as we forgive.'"

It took time, but in the loving setting of a mending basket church, the yarn of God's love began filling in the hole in that suffering soul.

Only love can reach into the "Ground Zero" of our lives and bring beauty out of ashes.

Once again, the time came to leave the open places and wing my way across the miles of valleys, lakes and mountains to a remote village where women had gathered for a time of refreshing.

Someone whispered, "Is there forgiveness for me? I destroyed my husband's career, broke up two homes, please tell me there is forgiveness for me."

"There is a balm in Gilead that heals the sin sick soul." The memory of that old song stilled my spirit before I answered.

"You must go back to the fork of the road," I answered quietly. "You must return to the place where you took the wrong turn and repent and ask forgiveness. Ask for God's grace and mercy to make your present home a safe place."

I know how difficult the road back can be. It is so easy to run, and such a long way to return to the fork of the road, but that is where the healing begins. I grieve for those who break God's rules, and then have to face the consequences of even forgiven sin, but the grace and mercy of God can weave a thick thread of love to heal the tattered places of the heart.

Those who have been forgiven much will love much, and I have seen healing of broken places by those who have learned much.

Just as Mama wasted nothing out of the missionary barrel, so God wastes nothing that comes out of the barrel of life. He alone can take the broken pieces and make something beautiful out of them.

Winging my way homeward, I thought of the old hymn, "I'm so glad I learned to trust in Him." I said, "Thank you" to the God I trusted as a six year old, and yes, He has been with me all through these 89 years, and He will be with me to that "Going Home" time.

In the distance, I saw the lights of the Wilmington airport, and for a moment I wondered how many miles I had to go "before I sleep." The shadows of the evening began to cover my home with a blanket of night. Unpacking my suitcase could wait for the morning. Before going to bed, under my down comforter, I had to sit quietly with my worn Bible, yellow with age and tears, a gift from my beloved husband, 65 years ago.

I read about a long ago time when Jesus sat around the table with his friends. Quietly Jesus said, "One shall betray me."

Judas went out and it was night, the night of the soul.

There was another time when his friend, Peter said, "I don't know Him." The day came when he wept, and he turned to see the look of compassion, and it was that look that turned Peter into a bold giant.

When Peter walked the shores of Galilee, I wonder if he had thoughts like these:

> *I should have known He needed me to watch and pray,*
> *but we had traveled far; it had been a long day.*
> *I should have brushed the Master's gown,*
> *when He fell upon His knees, but I turned to lie down.*
> *I should have wiped the blood drops, like tears,*
> *and stayed awake that night, to comfort through the fears;*
> *I should have loved, prayed, wept with him.*
> *The molten moment passed and never came again.*

— M.T.J.

Come, read with me where we come to the cross and the answer comes to us, "Forgive them, Father." For a moment He was forsaken so that we might never be forsaken.

Across the corridors of time we hear, "For God so loved the world, that He gave His only begotten son that whosoever believeth in Him should not perish but have everlasting life." (John 3:16)

It was another "Ground Zero" that Good Friday, when God's son paid the debt we couldn't pay, a debt He didn't owe. Then He cried, "It is finished!" God took that cry out of "Ground Zero" and turned it into Easter, with the cry "He lives!"

Chapter Nine

Uncle Barney

"Grammy, I thought you were going to tell me a story about Uncle Barney; here's a picture of him, handsome. I'll never get these albums finished; and then you want me to help you organize your books."

"Believe me, Sarah, if we ever get the albums and book-shelves organized, we'll have it made. My father should see my bookshelves: murder mysteries mixed in with theology, historical books beside fiction. On the top shelf, I keep the biographies of great leaders, wonderful reading."

When you read biographies of great people, you are reminded that into each life at some point comes a "Ground Zero," a time when dreams and hope tumble into a heap; then you read that out of the ashes, God brings forth a life of triumphs.

We never would have heard of Chuck Colson if there had not been a Watergate and a prison. Through it all God moved disaster to triumph by His amazing grace.

Joni Erickson would have been just another name, but God turned the wheelchair into a pulpit and a message of hope has been heard around the world.

We never would have heard of Corrie Ten Boom, nor would there have been a movie called "The Hiding Place," if there had not been the "Ground Zero" of the concentration camps. Out of that tragedy, the world heard a message of God's amazing grace.

"Lives of great men all remind us we can make our lives sublime. Departing, we leave behind us footprints in the sands of time." (Longfellow)

"What about Uncle Barney?"

His Norwegian name was *Bjarne*, but we called him Barney. He was not our real uncle, but he loved us and we loved him. To us he was always, "Uncle Barney."

Since he was partially bald, he wore an old felt hat that he tipped to the side; then he would thrust his hands into the pockets of a long black coat, fake a menacing glare and with his big brown eyes, he looked to us like a gangster. There was something wild about him, a part of the world "out there" we knew little about.

He had been a journalist in Norway, deeply in love with a fisherman's beautiful daughter. When she was lost at sea and his life turned to shambles, he sailed to Canada where he spent his days in riotous living; wine, women and song. In Winnipeg, he had an encounter with my Norwegian Papa. As a result of that, he knelt down beside the parlor sofa and changed direction from his way to God's way. He handed Mama the whiskey bottle, and when I asked Mama what she did with the whiskey, she smiled, "That's my business." Mama's meatballs were the best.

For hours he would entertain us with stories, songs and a strumming mandolin. We didn't understand why he couldn't repeat the song and stories until years later, when we realized he made them up as he went along.

He was dashingly handsome and the women fell in love with this mandolin musician. He followed our family from Canada to Chicago and to New York and became the self-appointed guardian angel to protect these children. He also turned out to be a watchman over the most guileless, naive man I've ever known, our Papa. "*Bjarne*," Mama said one day, "You must settle down and marry a good wife."

"You are so right, Mama, but God gave me such a big heart. I can't help it that I love them all."

One day he did marry a solid, plain, hardworking woman,

who idolized him. Mama was pleased to see *Bjarne* settle down. Mildred was a good wife.

As the years went by, the restlessness of his lost love made him vulnerable to the charms of a casual acquaintance in New York's Central Park. The result, a broken marriage.

By this time we were grown and married, with families of our own but to us, no matter where we lived, he was our Uncle Barney. He was the one who made us laugh. He always had a nickel for a Good Humor ice cream bar; he strummed his mandolin and sang Norwegian folk songs for Mama while she baked her bread. He was there for us when we went away to school and had our families.

One day he came to us with his mandolin and sang to our children, Jan and Dan.

I had memories of him sitting out on the fire escape on the second-floor flat in Chicago. With his felt hat pulled back, he strummed his mandolin and sang with mournful sound, "Sometimes I feel like a motherless child, a long way from home."

I didn't understand it then. I do now. Years had gone by and now he sat in my kitchen, strumming and singing.

When the children were asleep, he told me the story of the "Ground Zero" in his life.

> Your wonderful Papa, the best friend I ever had. He knew how desperate and ashamed I was and I didn't dream my marriage could be repaired after my foolish escapade; and in the darkness of the soul, I could only think of one thing, oblivion!
>
> One night, I walked along the Brooklyn Bridge, then stood in silent stillness, and felt the blackness of my soul. Before long an arm crept around me, "Come! Time to go home, for a cup of coffee." A policeman watched us go arm in arm.
>
> Step by step, your Papa walked me through the valley of despair to hope, forgiveness and the restoration of a broken marriage.

"What happened after that, Grammy?"

"Barney and Mildred (who loved him dearly), went to California and spent the rest of their lives working with the homeless, the despairing and the lonely, broken people. They brought hope to them, the message of God's love that by His grace, life can be beautiful again. Now, they are Home!"

"He once told me that he had never met two people like Mama and Papa, who were so pure in heart, so innocent of the world, yet with such a depth of compassion for the lost and wounded sheep.

"All those biographies on the top shelf are stories of great people who have made a historical mark in the course of human events. Yet, my dear Sarah, there are millions around the world who change the course of just one person, a biography only God keeps on His shelf.

"I recall the day when I watched the funeral service honoring England's "Queen Mum," as she was affectionately called. The pageantry was majestic in beauty, the faces of the people revealed the love and respect they held in their hearts for this great lady of England, whose life spanned many years of much change.

"Music of the hymns of faith that also spanned the years filled the great cathedral. I was deeply moved as I listened to the triumphant music and it seemed to be a celebration of her faith, not an end, but a beginning.

"Near the conclusion of the service, one of the ministers read from the last page of the Pilgrim's Progress."

> *I see myself now, at the end of my journey; my toilsome days are ended. I am going now to see the head, that was crowned with thorns and the face which was spit upon for me. I have formerly lived by hearsay and faith, but now I go where I shall live by sight.*
>
> *Glorious it was to see how the upper region was filled with horses and chariots, the trumpeters and pipers, with singers and players on stringed instruments to welcome the pilgrims as they went*

up, and followed one another in at the beautiful
gate of the city.

"When they closed the service with 'God save the king,' I was back in Canada, standing in the big hall with Mrs. Dabson's third grade class, singing 'God Save Our Gracious King.' How fast the years go by.

"Only royalty on earth has pomp and pageantry, the horses and chariots, the trumpeters and pipers, but one day is coming when the saints will go marching in, not only the great giants of faith who have made a noble mark on our day, but there will also be a Barney. There will also be a Monroe with his mountain sheep and the lonely forgotten preachers in far away places who brought the wounded out of hiding. They come one by one to the beautiful gate of the city.

"Oh, Lord, I want to be in that number, when the saints go marching in."

Chapter Ten

———⇒•◦•⇐———

Pearls and Potatoes

During a shopping trip to Boston, Jan and I decided to stop in a jewelry store and I selected a strand of pearls for my granddaughter, Heather, as a gift for graduating from Brown University.

After completing medical school, Heather, and her husband, Matt, are in a residency program at Cambridge, with no time for pearls. The practical perception of a frugal lifestyle for the moment, can obscure the reality that there will come a time for pearls. I wanted her to have them.

In my picture book of dreams, I can imagine Heather, dressed in a long shimmering gown, in the arms of her husband, entering a ballroom to celebrate the accomplishment of their dreams. In that moment, the white coats are temporarily put aside and the long hours of hospital duty become a memory. This is their molten moment and a time for pearls.

The thought of pearls takes me back to the day, forty years ago, when Harold gave me a gift of pearls. With the practical perspective of present needs, I thought, "oh, no, I need a vacuum cleaner." But I hid my dismay with a warm cheerful, "Thank you."

Harold is Home now, and whenever I wear the pearls, I say "thank you," from a deeply grateful heart. Vacuum cleaners have come and gone, but the pearls are still here. They are a reminder of a gift of love that is for always.

There were pearls on another day, when I was fourteen, a time when Papa was the pastor of the Norwegian Baptist Church in Chicago. It was up to God and Mama to rear the children. He was busy with the Lord's work. He preached fervently, rescued the perishing, brought home the homeless, but he never knew the value of a dollar. Mama always kept a tight budget. Papa was given ten cents for a cup of coffee and a sweet roll at the auto mart; and street car tokens so she would be sure he could get home from the library where he studied. If Papa had the money, it would go to the poor. We were rich, but not in money.

After the Sunday evening service, Lily Olsen, the treasurer, knowing Papa's generous heart, would give the salary to Mama.

One Sunday, when Mama was home, tending to a sick child, Lily gave the money to Papa. On Monday morning, on his way to the library, Papa felt the money in his pocket. Completely forgetting where it had come from, he found himself in front of a jewelry store.

Looking inside the window, he saw a string of pearls and went inside. "*O ja*, Mama is the most beautiful woman in the world and I have never bought her a present. So now, a present for Mama."

When Papa returned home, he gathered us all together and with a great fanfare he announced, "Now there is only one woman in all the world for me, and she is the most beautiful woman and I never bought her a present." Bowing low, he presented the jewelry case, "For you, Mama."

Mama opened the case and there was a strand of pearls. "Oh Papa, they are beautiful."

With our mouths open, we watched them kiss, right in front of us. Then, like a knight in shining armor, he left for the library.

Since I was the eldest, it dawned on me that Lily had given Papa the money and I cried, "Oh, Mama, the money, we don't even have potatoes."

With shining eyes and a wistful smile, Mama gazed at the pearls in the jewelry case, "*O ja*, so it is, but the Bible says, 'For everything there is a season.' There is a time for potatoes and there is a time for pearls. Today is the time for pearls!"

I don't remember how the potatoes came, but they were there to nourish the body. The gift of pearls nourished the soul for years to come. It was the only present Papa ever bought, but he gave her a lifetime gift, "In all the world there is only one Mama."

During the depression era, in the thirties, when I was in nurse's training, I would walk nearly five miles through Humbolt Park to get home and enjoy a free afternoon.

"What did you have for supper last night?" I asked my sister Grace.

"Potatoes fried in lard."

"Mama, what are you preparing tonight?"

"*O ja*, I have diced potatoes, and I'm making a thick cream sauce with canned milk; then I sprinkle parsley on top, a good meal, but I wish I had just ten cents worth of bologna."

I helped set the table, the coffee pot perked happily, and Mama had whole wheat bread, and a sugar lump. We were blessed.

In the meantime, Uncle Barney, with hunched shoulders, head bowed in hopelessness after looking for work, put his face to the wind and headed to Mama for a cup of coffee. He thrust his cold hands into his pockets and there he felt a dime tucked into the corner. He quickly turned toward the butcher shop. "Ten cents worth of bologna, sliced thin."

I had finished setting the table and Mama was stirring the cream sauce when we heard someone climbing up the stairs to the second floor. It was our Uncle Barney.

"Look, Mama, ten cents of bologna."

Mama fried the bologna and put it around the platter with the creamed potatoes. "For everything there is a season." That was the time for potatoes and bologna.

Sugar lumps were dipped in coffee; laughter blew through

the Chicago alley with the sound of hope.

Moments come like pearls, a reminder that there is a time for potatoes, but also a time for pearls; hope that springs up like a blade of grass through concrete. Hope slips in on the wind coming down a Chicago alley, hope that comes with ten cents worth of bologna and rides on laughter. Pearls nourish the soul long after the potatoes are gone.

One day, someone will open my jewelry case and remember, "For everything there is a season." Don't forget the pearls.

Chapter Eleven

━━━━◈━━━━

Queen Mary

Sarah, my granddaughter, sat on the floor of my office sorting through pictures to place in albums for all the grandchildren.

Her hair lay softly around her face while her large blue eyes questioned the pictures in her hand.

"Grammy, who are all these people?"

"I can tell you their names, and the families they belong to, but I'm ashamed to tell you I didn't take the time to know them."

"I've heard so many stories about the Norwegian grandmother, but don't know much about my Dad's grandmother, Elise Mogenson Jensen."

· · · · · · ·

Katie's middle name, Elise, was from her, while you were given Nightingale, from your mother's father, who was a Nightingale descendent. Yet, I know little about her past, a mistake on my part. I have a cousin in Seattle, Marty Hefty, who had done research about the Lund family in Norway, and your brother, Eric, has the Lund name. One of these days I will have to show Eric some of Marty's research.

"Here's a picture of your Danish great grandmother, Elise, in her garden in Arkansas. She is beautiful, tall and slender with white hair, holding roses. That's why we call her "Queen Mary." She always had that regal look and could be intimidating, but she did command respect. It took me years to learn to love her.

You know that Aunt Joyce and I married brothers. I married Harold and Joyce married Howard, eight years younger than Harold. We found out that Mama Elise thought that the descendants of the proud Danish Mogensons should marry Danes. She considered us Norwegians a notch below the marriage scale. The joke between the brothers was that she offered Harold $2,000 not to marry me, but offered Howard $3,000 not to marry Joyce. Now and then Joyce reminds me of her greater worth. Every once in a while the brothers would tease us and say, "We should have taken the money, these women are impossible."

After we were married, we received long letters on how to manage our home and children. I answered graciously but I'm afraid I kept my heart at a distance. One day I sent a special gift to Mama Elise, and she wrote Harold a beautiful letter thanking him for the excellent choice and added, "I could tell you picked it out." My Harold had a good laugh because he seldom wrote, forgot dates, and left it all up to me.

"When Uncle Jack, the eldest son, retired, he came to Wilmington to be near us, but until that time he lived with his parents in Arkansas; and I must tell you this, Sarah, he was a faithful son who cared for his parents until they died. Mama Elise managed to keep her *Eigle* (Jack) to herself. Fern and Harriet, the sisters, were married and lived in Chicago, and Mama's two favorite grandchildren were Fern's sons, Michael and Douglas."

Sometimes I think that the fears, hurts and circum-stances beyond control leave scars that cause people to reach, perhaps unknowingly, to the present where they can hold something or someone within control. Before Uncle Jack died, he told us a story about his early child-hood, and it seems to me that he grew "too soon old" when very young. That was probably due to his father working as a bricklayer away from home, and young Jack had to be the "man of the house."

It was June 29, 1920. Your Papa Harold was eight years

old and was sent out in the evening to bring the cows home. A frightening summer storm suddenly lashed out with thunder and lightening; then hail, larger than golf balls pounded on the roof where Mama Elise was in labor. Papa Jens was in another town laying brick, so Jack raced to get the midwife.

"Where is Harold?" Mama Elise kept crying. "He rode the horse to get the cows." In the midst of the storm the midwife came. While hail pounded the roof, Howard was born on Harold's eighth birthday. Suddenly Mama Elise cried out, "Harold is dead! No one can live in this hail out on the prairie."

She cradled her new son in her arm and wept bitterly. She had lost one son in birth some years ago and now she thought she had lost another son.

After the storm, morning came with a quiet calm. A horse came slowly to the barn; on his back young Harold lay sound asleep.

When Papa Jens returned, he had a son, Howard, and Elise's hair had turned snow white.

"How did you survive the dark night of the storm?" Papa asked.

"I stayed under the belly of the horse and he never moved and let the hail come."

Needless to say, horse and rider were inseparable. He added, "I got the cows home."

When I heard that story, I could better understand Mama Elise's unrelenting desire to hold her boys forever; but "what we grasp too tightly we lose, and what we loose we gain." I'm thankful that she finally was able to release her sons, even to two Norwegian girls, and we learned to love and appreciate her courage. Yet it was Aunt Joyce who won her heart. People have often asked me, "Who is the most like your Norwegian Mama?" My answer is always, "My sister Joyce." She seemed to have my mother's gentle, loving and understanding heart, along with godly wisdom.

When Mama Elise came with biting sharp words, I had a tendency to cringe and back away, but Joyce came to an understanding how to adjust to the situation. Since

Howard and Joyce lived in Arkansas at the time, they were able to see his parents more.

Instead of accepting the visits as a duty, as I often felt, Joyce made the time a challenge. She asked advice about small things, she also wrote down Mama's favorite recipes and listened to the "sermons" on religion; then she gently turned her attention to "whatever things are good." Music was a blessing to Mama Elise. Papa Jens would rock in his chair, his brown eyes sparkling with humor, for he knew how Joyce could turn the "sermons" into singing.

Every once in a while, Papa's sense of humor came through. One day Mama Elise was giving an exhortation and proclaimed, "Narrow is the road to salvation and few there be who find it, and my, how broad is the road to destruction." Papa interrupted and said, "Oh, come on Mama, it's not so bad since they paved it." Mama Elise doubled up laughing.

At another time, Papa Jens, who was getting forgetful, leaned over to me, while we were seated at the table with children and grandchildren, and asked, "Are all these mine? Where did they come from?"

"Yes, Papa, they are all yours and I have to admit you have some good looking sons." He looked around and with his delightful chuckle answered, "The girls aren't bad either." He shook his head, "I can't believe they all belong to me."

Joyce used her gift of steering Mama Elise away from criticism of the family to talking about God's love for all of us; then added, "Let's sing." One of her favorites was "We'll talk it over in the bye and bye; we'll talk it over, my Lord and I." Joyce would sing and her beautiful voice stilled the restless sea within Mama Elise.

When Mama Elise had her heart attack, it was Joyce who lovingly cared for her, kept her home in order, prepared nourishing meals, and sang and read to her. They walked in the garden together, while Joyce learned about plants and gardening. Across the flowerbeds, the music rolled on the summer wind. Her words became less sharp, the thoughts mellowed with the years, but it was Joyce who poured the love into the tattered places of the soul. Joyce held a special place in Elise's heart, a place, not even her children knew. Jack, she idolized, but Joyce, she loved.

One day, when we were living in Greensboro, North Carolina, I received a call from Jack, in Arkansas. "Margaret, I don't know what to do. We planned a trip to Florida; we are all packed and ready to go. It was something Mama had been looking forward to, but now Papa is sitting here too stubborn to move."

"I will not go to Florida," he shouted in the background.

"Let me talk to him, Jack. Now Papa what in the world are those two up to?"

"Florida, that's what they are up to. Well, I won't go."

"Tell me, Papa, would you like to come to me?" He chuckled delightedly as though we were in a conspiracy together.

"Now, Margaret, I would like that." In a short time they were on the highway heading to Wrightsville Beach where we rented a beach house. Papa, with a look of triumph, sat on the pier in his B.V.D.'s, the back flap blowing in the wind. "You are in your underwear, Grandpa," the grandchildren exclaimed. "Humph! I'm more covered than those silly people on the beach."

Mama Elise fried flounder in butter and I mixed the salad. While the potatoes boiled, we lingered over apple pie and coffee. When we rocked on the porch, I should have noticed the misty eyes that looked far across the waves that rolled to Denmark, her childhood home. Her heart was with the loved ones she had left behind. Now they were gone, and she never had a chance to say goodbye.

When Papa Jens refused to return to Denmark, Mama Elise took to the helm, like Captain Mogenson's daughter, set sail to the new challenge, determined to plow through whatever storm she encountered to bring the Jensen ship to a safe harbor.

It took time for us to get beyond the biting tongue and penetrating blue eyes to understand a will, like steel, to live a life of honor and integrity; to see beyond the steel, a heart of deep affection that somehow stayed too deeply hidden.

The display of love came in different ways, one way for

me, was her gift of a beautiful copper coffeepot from Denmark.

It took me too long to understand that she was giving me a symbol of her life in Denmark. Now that I am older, I can picture that life: beautiful blue Copenhagen china on handmade lace doilies, silver trays with lace, holding open faced sandwiches, Danish pastry, and servants, in crisp linen aprons, pouring coffee from the treasured copper pot. In giving me that coffee pot, she was giving the Norwegian, a part of Denmark as a love gift. I said, "Thank you" then; now, I would express my gratitude from the depths of a thankful heart.

For years, the shiny coffee pot had a place of honor on my shelf; then I decided to make it into a lamp for Harold. When I took the inside part away, I discovered a $100 dollar bill tucked in a corner! Today the lamp, in the den, is a constant reminder of our limited understanding of people around us.

My Norwegian Mama didn't live in the rural south, but learned to blend with the culture of Brooklyn and Chicago. She did it with a compassionate heart of love, demonstrating God's love in a broken world

One day, she gave me a vase made in Norway, with many small pieces of blue and grey porcelain put together to make a work of art. Today it sits on a table in the living room that goes to Janice, our eldest, as a reminder that God, the Master potter, can put the generations together to create something beautiful. God sees the big picture, we see the broken pieces.

The Mamas were different, but God used the life of each as part of His plan.

I also realized that Mama Elise knew the rural South could not fully accept anyone coming from a "fer piece," but she earned the admiration and respect for her faithfulness in the Baptist church, and her joyous good humor. Her gardens became a tourist attraction that made her "famous." She entered into the plans of homecomings and revivals, but no one ever saw "Queen Mary" in a feedsack dress. When she brought food to a tea, they were Danish open-faced sandwiches, and cookies made with butter. There were limits to adjusting.

One evening when the sun cast its lingering gold over the sound, Mama Elise turned to me and said, "I loved my children too much, too hard, held them too close. I want you to know how much I love you both, but I hope you don't mind if I love Joyce a little more. She's part of my heart. There are many things I'd like to say. I didn't always do things right. I just don't know how to say it, but I do love Joyce most."

I put my arms around her, "You don't have to say anything. I understand."

"Oh, another thing, Margaret, I told the family that if I should have a stroke, and I do have high blood pressure, that Margaret would take care of me. You see, the others fall apart, but you are like me, you know how to face storms."

"Mama, you know I'll take care of you, since I am the nurse in the family."

"I know," she replied softly and looked at me as though she had bestowed on me a great honor, and she had. It was then I really loved her.

"Well, my darling Sarah, I've been telling you a long story, and we didn't get any albums finished. That was the last time we were together. In September, we received the call that Mama Elise had gone Home. I remembered that it was Papa's stubbornness that had given us the most remarkable time at Wrightsville Beach."

Uncle Jack told us how Mama Elise was working in her garden, pruning roses, when she dropped her pruning shears and called Jack at work. "*Eigel* come quickly. I am going Home." When Jack came down the road, he stopped for the doctor and together they went inside. Mama Elise was on the sofa. She looked up with a beautiful smile and went Home.

Michael, the grandson, found the pruning shears on the ground. "Now, I know she was pruning her roses because she never left her shears on the ground, always up on the ledge."

She was buried at the country church in Benton, Arkansas, where we sang her favorite songs. I recalled a time when I walked with her in the garden and she stopped and looked up, "Margaret, can you hear it?"

"Hear what, Mama?"

"The music, oh it is so beautiful, surely you hear it."

I didn't hear anything.

"Margaret, can't you smell the roses?"

"Oh, yes, your roses."

"No, the fragrance of Heaven," and she took a deep breath, "Oh, Margaret, the roses of Heaven, surely you can smell the fragrance of Heaven."

I looked at Mama Elise, the one who loved us both (but Joyce the most) and I could almost hear the music of Heaven and almost smell the fragrance of Heaven.

Her triumphant smile, in death, shouted to the world, "I won. The captain's daughter won. O, grave where is your sting? I am Home with my beloved ones, the Mogensens, more than that I am Home because I'm a child of the King."

Jesus said, "Let not your heart be troubled, I've gone to prepare a place for you."

"There's a land that is fairer than day, by faith we can see it afar."

Mama Elise saw the fair land, smelled the fragrance of Heaven, and heard the music. She left earth with a smile.

· · · · · · ·

Sarah closed the albums; tomorrow was another day.

These days should be remembered
throughout every generation. Esther 9:28
Tell your children. Joel 1:3

The pictures you see are real people; some are world famous who
Brought hope around the world.
Then again, we, the ordinary, do the everyday tasks within our hand,
A cup of coffee, a loaf of bread, a song, a story, shared tears and joy; yet
God takes the
Tangled yarn and weaves hope in a broken world.
Faces with the stories....

Janice Carlberg, Ruth Nelson, Eldred Nelson Bjarne Langmo, Ruth Langmo, Jud Carlberg. We were together when our world changed forever. 9 /11 /01.

Dr. and Mrs. Eldred Nelson, Seattle, Washington. Stitching hope through camp meeting songs.

Sarah Jensen Howard, "Who are these People?" (The Albums.)

Bill Bright brought John 3:16 *to the world & founded* Campus Crusade — *Now Home. Les Stobbe, President of* Here's Life Publishers, *brought hope through books.*

Jim Warren (The golden voice of Prime Time America Moody), Margaret Jensen, Jean Warren (Jim's lovely wife) and Harold Jensen.

Lena Leach — "Unclog the channel with praise. Pray the promises — not the problem."

Bjarne Hoiland — Uncle Barney & the Tweten children. (10 cent bologna)

Leona Holvick, 42 year old nurse who married The Mountain Man (22 years old) and stitched hope throughout the Mountains for 50 years.

Wedding day of Monroe (22) and Leona (42)

Monroe Holvick, The Mountain Man. The happy Mountain Man.

Harold, Margaret, Leona and
Monroe. The trip to the Mountains.

The Jensens Golden Wedding Anniversary.

Jens Jensen and Elise Mogenson Jensen (The Captain's daughter)

The sisters: Jeonelle, Doris, Margaret,
Joyce and Grace. (Last picture together.)
Jeonell, Doris and Grace — Home!

Howard & Joyce Jensen (Joyce & I
married brothers). Home, 2000;
Harold, 1991

The White Haired Warriors:
Joyce Solveig Jensen & Margaret
Jensen.

Sarah and Aunt Joyce.

1899 — Elvina Leonora Johnson (15 yrs. old.) and Bertilda Johnson (her Mother, our
Grandmother).

1917 — Going to church horse and buggy —
Papa, Mama and baby Margaret Tweten.

1918 — The Twetens – Margaret,
Papa and Mama.

Elvina Leonora Johnson Tweten (her story is in First We Have Coffee*) She walked with God. He took her Home in 1977.*

1919 — Bernice (baby) Mama and Margaret (2 yrs. old)

1937 — Harold & Margaret.

1988 — Harold & Margaret.

Four generations — Heather, Jan, Margaret and Mama Tweten.

Four generations — Jan Carlberg, Margaret, Lily Willis and Heather Carlberg Willis (Now Dr. Heather).

Ralph and Christine Jensen.

1980's — The Jensen family. Left to right: Jud Carlberg, Chad C. Heather, C. Jan (Jensen) Carlberg, Ralph Jensen, Chris Jensen, Eric J. Shawn J. Jensen, (Kathryn) Elise Jensen and Sarah J.

1991 — The Jensen family. The last picture with Harold.

2000 — The Jensen family at the Beach House.

The Carlbergs: Jud Carlberg, Jan (Jensen) Carlberg, Lily, Willis, Chad C., Dr. Matt Willis and Dr. Heather C. Willis.

Chad Carlberg — No. 1 Grandson.

Heather Carlberg Willis (Now Dr. Heather) and Grandmother.

Scarlet — I'm in charge here! *My Office.*

Paul Howard Jensen with Son, Stephen Jensen (Air Force Pilot).

Steve Jensen (Air Force Pilot) and Sister, Krysta.

Chad Marschewski — Iraq.

Jim & Judy (Jensen) Marschewski's adopted sons in the military: Joslin, Jeffery, Jess and Chad.

Jeff Marschewski — Iraq.

*Christine & Ralph with son Eric —
Afghanistan.*

Christopher Shawn Jensen — Iraq.

*From land, sea and sky, our youth stitched the light of
freedom's hope into the darkness of tyranny.*

(Kathryn) Elise Jensen — Iraq.

*K. Elise Jensen — Hope springs up
in Iraq.*

Sarah (Jensen) and Tommy Howard.

Christopher Shawn Jensen & Deva.

Chad and Kristina Carlberg.

Drs. Heather, Matt and Willis and Lily. (Stitching Healing Hope in an Arizona Reservation.)

Lilly and Luke Willis.

Great Grandma La La with Luke & Lily.

Eric-Clover Jensen (wife) Gracynne-Lund.

Chapter Twelve

A Safe Place

When the alarm went off at 4:30 a.m., I reached over to the night table to push a button that would put an end to that piercing sound. I wrapped a soft robe around me and gravitated to the coffee pot that had been set the night before; then turned up the heat to dispel the morning chill and wondered what in the world was I doing in the darkness, just before dawn.

For some reason I recall reading that this hour before dawn is our "lowest point," when people die in their sleep; so it was with my Harold when he went Home, his highest point, my lowest. He went Home to Heaven's dawn in a safe place, where tears are wiped away, and he knows the reality of what we believe by faith, that it really is worth it all to choose God's way.

I was left with the low point of how to keep living with part of you in a safe place, yet I was left to watch the towers of power fall to a storm of hate and no safe place — or was there?

There were other times when I was awakened in the darkness before dawn, not by the insistent clamor of a bell, but by an inner call to prayer: my lamb was lost in a culture that had no safe place.

"The shepherd went out to search for the sheep and all through the night on the rocky steep. He sought 'til he found him; with love bands he bound him. My son was that one lost sheep."

I sat quietly in the stillness of that hour before dawn, and gave thanks. My son was safe in the fold, but there were other sheep, lost in the far country.

It was then I remembered Mama Elise's storm cellar on the farm. "Come, Margaret, let me show it to you." On the outside wall, below the kitchen, she opened a lid and hooked it onto the wall so the wind wouldn't blow it on top of us, and we descended into the murky darkness, illumined by the kerosene lamp. Shelves were lined with canned goods, potatoes and carrots were tucked into beds of sand, stored for the winter; blankets rolled up on a shelf had to be aired out periodically; folding chairs, table and metal containers held non-perishable food, first-aid kit, candles and matches.

· · · · · · ·

Sometimes we can sense a storm; the animals are restless, the birds disappear into safe places, then a strange cloud seems to slip up with a sinister warning.

One day we heeded that warning about an impending storm. Within moments children were urged into the storm cellar; then I grabbed what I could before I descended the ladder, the men eased in just as the roar came toward us. The house might blow away, but deep in the murky darkness, in the bosom of earth, for this moment we were safe.

We waited, listened and prayed for the wind to pass, then carefully the men opened the heavy lid, one by one we crawled out to view the disaster. We saw a path of broken-off trees like fence posts cut with a saw. Stories came to us about animals, wagons, machinery, even houses that were sucked up in a funnel, and then deposited some other place. A neighbor's cow landed in our pasture. Chickens, dead or alive, seemed to be everywhere. Houses and buildings, in the fury's path, were leveled; then another building inches away was not touched.

Our house was spared that time, so we set about to prepare meals and shelter for the present, while the community confronted a plan for the future rebuilding.

Believe me, Margaret, sitting in that storm cellar makes us realize the importance of keeping short accounts with God and each other. It's not how many times a storm knocks us down, but how many times we get up. It seems to me some folks get more than their share of "knocking down," but they seem to be the ones who call to others, "Come, get up; we did it, so can you."

Then again sometimes the knocking down can destroy a man; like the time, out west during a typhoid epidemic, when a farmer stopped his wagon at our place. "My wife and five young-uns in the wagon died from typhoid." After the burying, he disappeared, grief too much to bear.

. . . .

I sat with my cup of coffee, remembering Mama Elise and understanding what made her the proud "Queen Mary." It was her way to survive. I also thought of my own Norwegian Papa who seemed too stern and unapproachable. He had seen six deaths in his family before he was nine years old; then he was sent to strangers to work on the farm for room and board.

When he was almost eighty he shared a story with me about how he used to help his Mother dig potatoes when he was four or five years old; then she would stop and say, "Shush, stop and listen to the song of the potato bird." He said, "We stood hand in hand listening to the song of the potato bird. After all the deaths of my family, I would run from the farm where I was working to the empty home place and call out 'Mor Mor' (Mother) and I seemed to hear her say, 'Shush, stand still and listen to the potato bird.' I was comforted.

"When I was fifteen someone invited me to a home prayer meeting and there I learned that God loved me and had a plan for my life. Later I came to Chicago to study at Chicago University. Just think, after forty years in America, I could go back to Norway, and Margaret I went to the potato patch and heard again the song of the potato bird. *Ja, ja*, so it goes, Margaret. The heart finds a safe place." I understand him better now, and only wish I could have had a listening heart many years ago."

There is something mystical about the darkness before dawn, when memory rolls like a rerun of life in living color and the color improves with the years.

Now it was time to turn off the coffeepot, and get dressed; for dawn had slipped in softly, not like "Thunder across the bay," but as a gentle reminder that a new day had begun. Within a short time I was on my way to an early breakfast to hear Elizabeth Dole, our next senator from North Carolina.

There didn't seem to be an extra inch of space in the community clubhouse. Tables were filled up with friends from around the country, not only for the southern breakfast of grits, sausage and biscuits, but they came for the honor of meeting Elizabeth Dole in person.

While waiting for her entrance, I had an opportunity to observe the audience around me; middle-aged couples, young people, and some folks, like me, with white hair. There seemed to be more men, but then politicians do stand out, with their white shirts and red ties. I'm used to sizing up an audience and it seemed to me that these were the same people I see around the country, in churches, conferences or retreats. They represented a "heap of living." I also know that sometimes smiles hold at bay tears that are close to the surface. We all say, "Just fine, thank you," but the "Ground Zero" of broken dreams, dashed hopes, grief over straying sheep, stay just below the surface of a brave smile.

"Life is what happens to you while you are making other plans." I learned that when I worked in the emergency room as a nurse.

Sometimes, when I sit on a platform and view the attractive audience in front of me, I wonder if I tell them enough about storm cellars for the storms of life. Am I wise enough to detect a swallowed sob in a "Fine, thank you"?

"Make me an instrument of Thy love," hangs on the wall in beautiful embroidery. "Oh, God, let that desire be imprinted on my heart."

I heard the joyous crowd around me sharing news of children in school, sports and church, or "Will the azaleas be ready for the festival or will the gardens be rained on during the parade of homes?" Looking around I saw America, the real grass roots Americans, going to work, mowing their lawns, figuring taxes before the deadline, building strong families and getting up in the dark before dawn to show support of a leader of honor to represent us in Washington.

Suddenly my thoughts are interrupted and the doors open. "The next Senator from North Carolina, Elizabeth Dole."

The crowd stood with thundering applause and it seemed that every man became a Kentucky Colonel, ready to tip his hat to the gracious, charming Southern Lady. Behind that beautiful lady is the tested steel of moral courage, integrity, character and honorable service to our country. Her spontaneous humor was contagious, but the challenge to pray for our nation, President and leaders was a reminder that this was our hope out of "Ground Zero."

"I'm counting on Prayer Warriors across the country, for without God we can do nothing."

During the endless line of handshakes, I heard, "We are praying for you, God bless you." This is the real America!

When I pulled into my driveway, I noticed a touch of spring bringing my azaleas to life; they will open for the Azalea Festival. I did get my taxes done. I'll have Sunday dinner as usual; this time, roast beef and mashed potatoes. Character is built in the everyday, mundane tasks of living where no one sees us.

My Norwegian Papa is right. "*Ja*, we are what we have been becoming."

The day came to an end and I sat in the quiet with a cup of tea and my faithful Doberman across my feet.

"Please stay," she was saying. I'm doing more of it, staying, listening, and just maybe I can hear the song of the potato bird. Before I closed my eyes, I sang an old hymn. (I do that often, sing myself to sleep.) "He hideth my soul in the cleft of the Rock and covers me there with His hand." My safe place, God's storm shelter.

Chapter Thirteen

Uncle Jack

I heard his cane tapping on the driveway so I put on the teakettle. "Time for a break," he announced, and that meant I had to leave my unfinished writing on the desk and stop for a morning visit. Uncle Jack's favorite topic was to expound on the rearing of children in our day. Since he was an eighty-five year old bachelor, he had the answers, "Too much sports. Yes, they need to study more, and spend more time in church."

At my sister's suggestion, I switched the subject to stories from the past. It worked! As he spun tales from Denmark, I had a new appreciation of the courage of Harold's parents to embark on a journey to a new world and leave the familiar behind.

The Mogensons were sea-faring people from father to son; ships' captains who sailed around the world. What tales they could have told if we had been there to listen — but most of the stories are buried in a sea of silence. I found that these strong Scandinavian forefathers kept their own stories hidden, but told great tales of adventure by others. Little by little, I was able to get a picture of the hopes and dreams, courage and fears of a generation before us, who dared to live life with their faces to the wind.

Later in the day, Kathryn Elise asked about her great grandmother, Elise Mogenson, who married Jens Jensen, the dashing, handsome architect from Copenhagen.

. . . .

Uncle Jack told me that Elise was incredibly beautiful; an artist did an oil painting of her when she was sixteen and for many years it hung in an art gallery.

Mama Elise told me how her father, the ship's captain, upon returning from the sea, would play a pirate game with her. He roared that he would catch her and take her out to sea; then she would run in the fruit orchard and call, "Come and find me, Pirate," and they went round and round until he caught her up in his arms, laughing and tickling her with his beard. She apparently had an idyllic childhood, with orchards and gardens to play in, seaside trips and household servants to care for the family.

Elise fell in love with the dashing architect, who had flashing brown eyes, dark wavy hair and a black curling mustache; also he was several years older. When she was eighteen, they married, and Jack, weighing thirteen pounds, was born nine months later; two years later, Aunt Harriet was born, a beautiful blue-eyed blonde. The other children were born in America.

One day Jens Jensen announced to his Elise that since he had completed a long project, it would be an adventure to visit his brother in America before he went back to the drawing board with plans for a new building.

Elise was beautiful, tall and slim, about five feet and six inches, clear blue eyes, fine classic features, soft blonde hair pulled back with a bow. Her fun-loving, free spirit went along with the challenging adventure: a trip to America. In high spirits, the young family boarded the ship to America, and encountered the worst storm in history. "You know Margaret," Elise told me in her soft Danish accent, "That poor Jens was so sick, stayed down in his cabin, throwing up and praying to die." I took my babies up on deck, *Eigle* (Jack) was three, Harriet was one, and told them, "Now you remember, you are Mogenson, sea-faring people and Mogensons don't throw up. So don't you dare throw up." They didn't!

It wasn't until just before Uncle Jack died that we heard the rest of the story. When they landed on shore, Jens announced, "I will never, no never, cross the ocean again."

No one knew why they never returned to Denmark, to family and friends. Mama Elise never mentioned it and refused to return alone. A commitment was a commitment and she stood by her man.

One day she said to me, "I found myself in America, on a farm in Nebraska, living with my brother-in-law and his family. We had servants in Denmark. I was the spoiled daughter of Captain Mogenson, so I said to myself, "Elise, if Jens thinks that this is the life for me, well, we will just see about that.""

Poor Papa Jens, the dashing Dane, didn't realize that there was no market for an architect who couldn't speak English, too stubborn to admit he was wrong, so he designed his own creative way to lay bricks. Elise had studied English in Denmark, but now she devoured books in the library, searched the newspapers for employment, then she found an escape. "A banker needs a manager for a large farm in Nebraska." The captain's fun-loving daughter took the job. Jens, no longer an architect, became a farmer and a brick layer.

You know, Kathryn Elise, we really have to admire his courage to go along with the idea, but that is what challenges do, they propel us into places we've never been.

Papa Jens laid bricks and took care of the buildings. Mama Elise went to all the farmer's meetings, devoured agricultural literature and even won a debate about Abraham Lincoln. She also hired the help, ran the farm, milked the cows, raised a garden and chickens, and brought three more children into the world.

Your great grandmother Elise, was bigger than life and filled the home with her optimism and her loving spirit that flowed in her children. In looking back, I can see what made her seem so controlling and intimidating. It was a role she had thrust upon her when life hit "Ground Zero." She was after all, Captain Mogenson's daughter.

"Margaret," she said to me one day, "The difference between a general and a private is that a general makes things happen, a private lets things happen." If I had known the past, I would have understood the roles these grandparents played. Mama Elise was the general, not because she asked for it, but because circumstances tossed the role to her. On the other hand, Jens gave up on being the dashing architect, but accepted what he thought couldn't be changed, and allowed circumstances to shape him.

Mama Elise had no need for self-esteem seminars. She invented self esteem! They never stopped loving each other, but I think she realized that she lived with a man with broken dreams, yet they were a team, united by a commitment to God and each other for fifty-eight years.

No wonder the Bible says, "Judge not," because only God knows the places of the soul that needs mending.

I miss Uncle Jack's tapping cane coming down the driveway. Now they are all Home and the stories are for you to tell the next generation, Kathryn Elise. I miss the cup of tea and raisin toast, and I miss the stories. But most of all, I miss the times we spoke of God's faithfulness.

In spite of all the cups of tea with Uncle Jack, I really never knew him until after he went Home (He died peacefully in his sleep.) It was then, at the memorial service, that young people stood up to tell of the lasting influence their "Uncle Jack" had on their generation. "I wouldn't have made it if he hadn't encouraged me." "He gave me hope," and said, "You can do it." "He was a faithful friend to a pastor," I kept hearing the word, "faithful," even his doctor wrote, "What a Southern Gentleman."

So my dear Kathryn Elise, we often judge people by their outstanding accomplishments, yet the small acts done in secret, the person you are when no one is looking, that defines a person!

One day God will say, "Welcome Home, good and faithful servant."

· · · · · · ·

Another day had come to a close, the albums set aside for another day. I reached for a cup of tea, and feel a sadness, like a poet said, "Like a mist following rain," and recalled how I thought that Uncle Jack's "Time for a break" was an interruption in my well planned day; then as time went on, I saw it as "Divine intervention."

Those molten moments brought stories from the past and a time to reflect on God's faithfulness through all generations. I regret that I yielded too often to the "tyranny" of the "urgent," rather than to realize the path we are on will wait while we get the stone out of our shoe. Only once did he hint at a "Ground Zero" in his life when he told my grandson, Shawn, "Follow your dreams, it's too lonely to be alone." From that distant dream, he brought hope to others.

In quietness there is strength, so I'm sitting quietly on the porch swing, holding a cup of tea. I realize that I, too, need the "mending basket;" the yarn of understanding that brings renewed hope for the next generation.

I miss the tapping of the cane!

Chapter Fourteen

Homecoming

"Doesn't anyone in this house stop for lunch?"

"We're in the office, Dad. Grammy's on the phone and I'm working on albums, trying to organize these pictures."

Ralph winked at me, and then gave Sarah a hug.

"How about a grilled cheese, Dad, and there are cokes, and chips, maybe pickles."

"Sounds great."

Sarah bounced off to the kitchen while I concluded my phone conversation. "That was an invitation to a 'Homecoming' dinner on the grounds, and all-day singing." I put the phone down and turned to Ralph who had spotted a picture of Grandpa Jens. Ralph remembered, "When Grandpa got old he couldn't remember who we were, especially me. He used to say, 'Now who do you belong to?'"

"Papa, I am Harold's boy." Then he asks, "Harold? Who is Harold? Oh, there he is, yes, yes, that's my boy."

I began telling Ralph about that afternoon when I took the picture of Grandpa Jens, sitting on a bench in the backyard, with a shawl over his bony knees; his dog, Buddy, at his feet and his cane beside him. His white hair framed his weather beaten face and his once strong hands, now thin and blue veined, lay folded across the shawl. His brown eyes, now dim, looked out across the gardens.

I snapped the picture then sat beside him. "Papa are you talking to yourself?" He chuckled, "I'm talking to Buddy." We sat for a moment in silence. Mama Elise had gone Home five years ago.

He shook his white head and wistfully said, "Why did Mama have to go and leave me? Who will cut my toenails?" He looked around the garden. "She's here, always in the garden, so I talk to her."

· · · · · · ·

Sarah called from the kitchen, "Grilled cheese now served; cokes, pickles and chips."

I closed the office door, my safe place, a beautiful room in back of the garage, spacious enough to serve as a guest room if necessary, but a safe place for my untouchable papers.

When we entered the breakfast nook, Sarah had lunch ready, also a deep purple Iris in the vase. "You always seem to find the first touch of spring, Sarah, and you are one creative young lady. I was telling your Dad about the picture, Sarah, but I didn't finish the rest of the story."

· · · · · · ·

I know Papa Jens was far away in his thoughts, but I asked him if it was true that he bought the farm in Colorado, without Mama Elise knowing about it.

"Sure did," he chuckled. "Mama didn't like it but I had to show her I could buy land. I used my extra money from bricklaying. That banker in Nebraska, who owned the land we managed, gave Mama half of my salary and said, 'I know who runs this farm.' He was right but I didn't like it, so I decided to surprise Mama with a good deal. Besides I didn't have to deal with the banker, now we were on our own. Can't remember much of it now, but I guess we managed."

· · · · · · ·

The rest of the story would come later. We sat in the breakfast nook, looking out of the bay window to the woods where a touch of spring was pushing the dead leaves to blow away in the wind.

"'When winter comes,' my Norwegian Mama used to say, 'Then the next thing to come is spring; then come the blue birds of promise.' By the way, Ralph, that phone call was about another homecoming in the mountains."

"You heard that, Sarah, your Grammy wants me to take her to another homecoming. Believe me, she could write a book about homecomings. The last time I took my Mama, we kept winding around country roads and I said, 'You really don't have to do this since you are putting the final touches on a book, and probably a small church with only forty members.'

"I know, but I promised two years ago and I can't go back on my word."

"Sarah, that is the same thing she told me the time before that. Mama has to learn to say, 'No.' You can see what a problem I have, not enough to keep my children in line, but I also have a mama who can't say 'No.'"

"So what happened last time, Dad?"

"We kept winding down the country road until we came to a small white church. When we pulled into the gravel parking lot, a breathless woman ran up to the car. 'I can't believe it, oh I can't believe it. You came to our church and we only got forty members.'

"Sarah, I thought your Daddy would explode. He tried so hard not to laugh: then the woman added, 'But we've got a crowd today, a hundred!' Your daddy eased out of the car, all six feet and six inches of him and he gave that sweet little old lady a hug and a 'God bless you,' and the hundred people fell in love with your Daddy."

Ralph looked out of the bay window over the woods into the Carolina Blue sky and added wistfully. "There was more to it than that, Sarah. The service was full of joy, with lots of Southern gospel music, and of course your Grammy had a story for the occasion, a true homecoming story about lost sheep coming home."

It was at the table, that I realized the importance of Homecoming.

. . . .

With plates piled high we sat around tables and met the visitors. One man was a C.E.O. from New York. "This is Grandma's church, so I fly in for Homecoming; never know when it is her last. She has been the rock in my life. I couldn't make it without her, and you'll never know what your story meant to me. I'm flying out this evening, so glad I could make it one more time. I know how much these people love each other and my Grandma, close to ninety, is surrounded by love. She is safe here."

Three attractive women also sat with us. "We came from this area. Now we are flight attendants from Colorado, but our grandmothers are here, and Homecoming is number one on our priority list. By the way I needed to hear what you said about the 'battle to believe.' It's a choice and like your Mama said, 'God's way is so simple, just not easy. You either believe the truth, or you don't believe. It's just that simple.' Thank you. We have the choice and we complicate God's simple message of love, so thank you. We have a flight to catch."

When they left Sarah, we visited with other families and met their relatives, and the young people gathered around Ralph to ask questions. "It's not cool to do drugs, just say No," I heard him tell a young man. One cute girl looked up at me with her big eyes and asked, "Is it a sin to wear bellbottoms?"

"Oh, I don't think so."

"Well, Ralph, where can I get some?"

"Honey, I don't know. You'll just have to ask her Mama." (Mama probably said "no.")

You should have seen your Dad, Sarah. The children called him "Ralph," like they had always known him.

At one time we sat at a table with a farmer and his three daughters and a son, a tall, handsome college graduate, and Ralph asked the son what his plans were and he answered that he wanted to farm with his Dad. Then he offered to take him on a tour of the farm in his new truck.

"I think that's great," Ralph told him, and added, "You're probably driving all the girls crazy."

I remember, Sarah, how that young man looked out over the fields surrounding the church on the corner. "I need someone like my Mom, one who loves the country like I do. Believe me, they are hard to find."

"You'll find her," I answered. "God has a plan for your life and He hears our prayers."

· · · · · · ·

"Thanks for lunch, Sarah, but I have a business to run; can't take all day for lunch."

Ralph picked up his car keys and went out the gate, whistling, "Country Roads Take Me Home."

I turned to Sarah, "Don't let him fool you, he loves those trips to 'Homecoming' and he'll take me."

It wasn't until after lunch when Ralph was gone that I could fill in some details that came from Uncle Jack when we had our ritual of tea and toast.

· · · · · · ·

It was true, Sarah, that Papa Jens bought the farm in Colorado and Mama was not pleased to leave Nebraska. To her it was a safe place.

I also learned that Papa Jens was almost eighty when he joined the Baptist Church. By that time he had heard enough sermons on 'broad is the road that leads to destruction,' that he decided to become a Baptist and line up on the narrow way and keep step with Mama Elise. He soon became the church's official greeter on Sunday morning.

Mama Elise told me how she dreaded the move to Colorado, knowing it was not a good choice. "But Margaret, I went."

Uncle Jack filled in the rest and told how Mama couldn't get her gardens to grow in Colorado. One day in utter frustration, she held up a fist of rocky soil and cried out to the heavens, "God, you can keep Your rocky land, and I refuse to plant one more bean in Your rocky soil, and I'm getting out of here."

That's when they sold our land and moved to Chicago where Papa Jens had a bricklaying job. They secured an apartment on Beach Avenue, near Humbolt Park, rent free, in return for managing the building.

Once again Mama Elise's organizational skills came into place. The Captain's daughter took over the helm until she went Home at the age of seventy-six. When Papa Jens died, at the age of ninety-three, he looked out over the gardens and smiled. 'Oh Mama, how nice of you to come,' then he was gone, buried beside Mama in Benton, Arkansas.

We miss his chuckle and gentle ways, his humor and even his stubbornness; but most of all his understanding heart.

· · · · · · ·

"I guess we can head back into the office where you can write, Grammy, and maybe I can get the albums organized." Sarah found her place on the floor surrounded by pictures, but when she picked up one photo, I knew there would be no writing today.

Chapter Fifteen

Monroe and Leona

"Who are these people, surrounded by goats and chickens?"

"My dear Sarah, forget the pictures. Get comfortable, for you are about to hear a mountain tale of long ago. That picture happens to be Leona and Monroe in the Ozark Mountains.

"Once upon a time, there was this preacher's daughter who was madly in love with a tall, blonde curly haired, blue-eyed young man; and he owned a Studebaker Coupe with snap on curtains."

"That sounds like you, Grammy. How old were you?"

. . . .

I was sixteen, but my father was strict and we could only go out in groups, so we were about twelve to four-teen young people who stuck together, went to the library, skated, played tennis and always went to church, where we sat together and wrote notes.

Monroe was part of the group; together we visited shut-ins, sang in prisons, and on Saturday night, we dished out soup and sandwiches to the homeless at the Pacific Garden Mission.

We had put on a program, told what God meant in our lives, and sang duets and quartets. I sang a solo: "No, never alone, no, never alone. He promised never to leave me, never to leave me alone."

At sixteen, I didn't have a clue what it meant to be alone, but I sang with my heart, because I knew that God would never fail anyone.

We gathered our music and headed for the street car; then had to transfer to the Fullerton Avenue Streetcar. While waiting for the next streetcar, Monroe got to telling a story, and he was good. In his enthusiasm, waving his arms, the transfers flew out of his hand into the Chicago wind.

We were frantic; no one had money, but we emptied our pockets and pooled our resources and came up with enough pennies to get us on board. By the time we boarded, we were hysterical with laughter; then the passengers joined in. It had to be good.

"The transfer blew away" Even the conductor was laughing. "But we made it."

"Where are you coming from?"

"We sang at the Pacific Garden Mission and fed the homeless."

"No kidding? Saturday, and you guys at a mission?"

"Come on sing." Before long the entire streetcar audience joined in.

Oh, come to the church in the wildwood.
Oh, come to the church in the vale.
No church is so dear to my childhood
as the little brown church in the vale.

We heard the bass voices, "Oh, come, come, come, come…" We made our exit to the sound of laughter and applause.

Now, Leona! She was a beautiful woman; a private duty nurse, and a talented musician, with a lovely soprano voice who often sang solos in my Papa's church. She made the world around her alive with her incredible energy and spontaneous humor, a dear friend of the family. To me, she was the "ideal nurse."

One Sunday morning, she was asked to sing a solo. On her way to the platform, the elastic in her bloomers broke and the embroidered drawers slipped to the floor. Without missing a beat, she slipped out of her drawers, rolled them up and tucked them inside, under her arm of her jacket; then proceeded to the platform. The pianist played the introduction and Leona sang her solo. "Nothing Between the Soul and the Savior."

Sometimes I think we must be Heaven's comedy show, for it seems to me there was more humor in Papa's church than any place I know.

I was madly in love with my Joe, so I recruited my friend for help. Leona, with her curly black hair and sparkling blue eyes, had a plan. She went to my father and told him that she had been offered a ride in a car so she wouldn't have to take the bus to Oak Park, and it would be nice to have Margaret with her. Could she go?

"*O ja*, how nice to get a ride."

Joe and I would take Leona home and make the return trip alone. We could stop for a cup of hot chocolate. What a perfect plan. We sat three in the front seat.

We said, "Good night" to Leona; I sat a little closer in the front seat of the remarkable coupe with the snap on curtains, when suddenly out of the back seat jumped my friend, Eleanor, "Surprise! Surprise!"

We never stopped for hot chocolate; the opportunity never came again. Later, cheerful Leona laughed, "Never mind, Margaret, I'll think of something." She did. But it wasn't what I expected.

Within a short time, when I was ready to enter nurse's training, Leona took me to Marshall Fields. She gave me a priceless gift, my first store bought dress, for my seventeenth birthday, along with silk hose and a pair of brown high heeled pumps. I was in heaven!

One day, she came with Monroe (the one who lost the transfers), and they asked Papa to marry them. Papa was in shock because Leona was forty-two and Monroe was twenty-two. Laughingly they said, "Don't worry; we'll celebrate a golden wedding anniversary. Just watch us!"

I was the bridesmaid at their beautiful wedding; and that's when I met your Papa. Harold and Monroe had been Boy Scouts together. Leona had thought of something!

After biblical training, and since Leona was a nurse, they volunteered to work in the Arkansas Ozark

Mountains under the Sunday School Union.

They found themselves living in a cabin, raising chickens and goats. Leona planted gardens, ran a clinic, and delivered babies. Monroe set up camp meetings, encouraged education, organized Sunday Schools and together they rode bicycles over rough trails and climbed mountains to visit the sick and needy.

Every now and then they drove their "beat up" car to visit Mama Elise and Papa Jens, who had retired to Benton, Arkansas, after their years of farming in Nebraska, Colorado and Michigan. Uncle Jack worked as an accountant of the *Reynolds Aluminum Co.*

Once again, Monroe, the master storyteller, entertained his audience with tales from the mountains.

· · · · · · ·

Now let me tell you about a Homecoming; might be poor as church mice, but when it comes to Homecoming, the best of everything comes out. Then there's the preacher's conference, and books should be written about those preacher stories. They get better every time you tell them, yes, sir, nothing in the world like Homecoming.

Now there was this church in the country, a fer piece, but the folks got ready. The treadle machines worked overtime when the women got a hold of Brother Otitis' feed sacks from the feed mill. Besides that, the recipes came out, and a feast was in the making.

Poor old Bo's Barber shop in that town yonder got business just before Homecoming when the women sent their men to get hair cuts, yes sir, the women did just that, after all it was Homecoming.

Hams hung in the smokehouse, farmers rendered sausage; the men eyed the chickens marked for Homecoming; even picked out a steer for butchering. Venison, when properly prepared could melt in your mouth.

Now, take Leona. We raised goats and she brought "a leg of lamb," all decorated fancy, and folks thought that it was the best eating, but it really was an old goat Leona doctored up.

It was hot, that day of Homecoming. Three preachers, all dressed up in black suits, white shirts and black ties, came with their best sermons. The other men came in clean overalls and new haircuts; you could tell because there was white against the sun-browned skin. You could see where the hair got cut. But it was the women; never saw such finery. Brother Ottis must have ordered new print feed sacks; oh, it was colorful!

The funeral parlor passed out fans, had "rest in peace," and the name Final Funeral Home (the owner's name was Fenwick Final, but that seemed too long). Those fans were mighty handy in that heat. The choir came marching in, almost like a city church. All the sopranos sat on the front row. Now Nettie and Mary Belle hadn't been speaking since Nettie did the solo in the Christmas pageant, but they let bygones be bygones, after all, it was Homecoming. The altos sat in the second row and Sally Sue (Pa liked Sue, Ma liked Sally) had her squalling young-uns on her lap.

The men came in, not too sure what they sang, but they would support the women any which way. Yes, sir, it was Homecoming. Their necks scratched from too much starch these fool women put in their shirts; even had to polish their boots. When women take a notion, might as well go along, believe me, when it comes to funerals, weddings, revivals and homecomings, women have the upper hand.

Oh, that choir could sing! "Hold Me, 'til the Storm Passes By" seems to be a favorite. I reckon they heard the story about the little boy who was so scared of storms, he just crawled up on his Pappy's lap, closed his eyes and said, "Pappy, just hold me 'til the storm passes by."

When the preacher got going, oh, it was hot. The fans from Final Funeral Home kept the air circulating: the soprano's skirts kept sliding up and the knees kind of come apart and there for all the world to see were the bloomers made out of Ottis' feed sacks; what a display!

About that time Sally Sue's young-uns let out a squeal and Sally Sue pulled out the nursing department; a contented baby fell asleep; then Sally Sue dozed, and the fan blew her blanket to the floor. Sally Sue's ample bosom was on display.

After three preachers, we were glad to hear the song leaders announce the closing hymn, "Victory in Jesus." The benediction included, 'Bless the hands that prepared this bounty;' and all the people joined in a hearty, "Amen."

The young-uns were grabbed by their ears, "Don't go ahead of the grown folks and remember your manners. This is Homecoming; friends and visitors are here, don't you shame us." Tables groaned under the platters of country ham, fried chicken, assorted vegetables from the gardens, sweet potatoes with brown sugar and pecans, venison, roasts, "leg of lamb" (Leona's goat) and pork chops.

Hettie could never understand why some folks in town don't cook their pole beans; eat them half raw. Pole beans aren't fit to eat unless cooked all day with fat back. Nothing like it, then there's the corn pudding and the pickles! Every kind of pickle showed up, but it was those crisp watermelon pickles that crackle and pop in your mouth that I can never get enough of. Yes, sir, it's the pickles that women fuss and stew over; about who makes the best.

Now, let me tell you about the desert table. I never saw anything like it; all those fruit cobblers. Bessie's coconut cake, "four stories high," she said. Then Lula brought her German chocolate cake; banana and strawberry pudding. There were all kinds of cookies. It was like a picture in a book.

There was enough food for an army; then one by one, the men found a shady place over by their trucks and dozed in between politics, crops, preachers and women in general.

The woman gathered their empty casserole dishes, shared recipes and planned for the next event. They found a shady spot, not to sleep, but to catch up on any news in the country. They knew the births that were due; counted the months after the wedding. Baptists were not to be disgraced.

Tears were shed over the friends who had "gone to a better place," but "how I miss Lillie Mae's apple pie. No Homecoming is the same without her apple pie."

What about sister May Belle? She wanted so much to

see her 100th birthday, died two days before. No one said "Amen" like Miss May Belle. Even when the preaching wasn't that great May Belle's "Amen" made us take notice that perhaps we missed something. That only made some preachers warm up.

The women sniffled together, remembering the chicken and dumplings Rose Ann made.

It'll never be the same without those dumplings and chicken. They got a mansion now, over the hilltop, but we sure miss them.

Look at it this way, Hettie, look at all the babies coming along, and a passel of young-uns here.

They brightened up, stopped sniffling, and said, "That's right. We got us a mission field right here. Most folks get saved and baptized when they are young; come right out of Sunday School."

"We better check on those white robes to be sure we are ready, and we need to look over the graves so no one goes unnoticed."

Looks to me like our work is never done; but the singers are getting lined up; the men seem to be stirring; nothing they like better than good quartet singing that comes from all over the country.

"I heard tell that way back in the hills in moonshine country, the folks don't know what goes on in the world. In fact, I heard that they didn't know there was a war going on until it was over."

"Didn't miss too much, the way I look at it."

"I heard this evangelist who came to one of the counties, all dressed up in a coat and tie; the farmers didn't like it because the women folk made the men dress up in white shirts.

"When you go up front to take up the offering, Zeb, you gonna look your best, hear?"

He heard!

Now, about that preacher who talked about how much God loves us and that He has a plan for each life. That's not all, but he told the young folks they could become anything they wanted to because the Bible says, "You can do all things because He strengthens you."

About that time folks got to figuring out that was meddling, not preaching. He didn't even take off his coat and tie, wave his arms and shout about "hellfire and brimstone." I always figured that revival time was to get folks scared enough about hell they'd be good Baptists. He said it didn't matter about being Baptists, Methodists or Lutherans, said that Jesus was the way, not a church.

That did it! That stirred up a hornet's nest and one old man said, "there you go; an educated preacher is like a drug store cowboy, ain't no account."

The preacher said, that God doesn't reach out with a big stick. The cross, a symbol of God's love through His Son, is the arms of God stretched out for us, not against us. I expect to see young people go out as nurses, doctors, lawyers, teachers, preachers and missionaries all over the world.

That's when they run him off! Yes, sir, that was too much, putting fool notions in young-uns heads, and next thing they'll leave their ma and pa and run off to be educated fools with no common sense. It takes hellfire and brimstone preaching to keep young people in line.

· · · · · · ·

"Now, Sarah, let me tell you something else: it was not the end of the story. Before the evangelist came no one had gone to college, many didn't finish high school, no missionaries in more than one hundred years. Fifty years later, I met some of those young people out of the hills: doctors, nurses, teachers, musicians and missionaries, all because someone put the seed of hope into their dreams."

"Oh Grammy, I can't believe all this is true."

"Of course it's true. As a young child, I sat at the table when preachers told stories and I soaked them up like a sponge."

"What happened to Leona and Monroe?"

"My father had a chance to visit them in the mountains, and agreed that they would probably celebrate their golden wedding anniversary."

"Did they?"

"Yes, they did! They were married fifty-three years; Leona was ninety-five when she died. Monroe died a few years later. God must have a hall of fame for people like Monroe and Leona who leave a trail of blessings that multiply along the way."

"We'll close up shop for another day, Sarah. I think it was Dennis the Menace who said, 'Tomorrow comes before I finish with today.'"

We closed the door to the office. The albums were left on the floor.

There would be more stories from the "Mountain Man."

Chapter Sixteen

The Mountain Visit

About fifty years ago, Harold and I decided to visit Leona and Monroe in the mountains. We rode the mountain trails they traveled, saw the schoolhouse and watched the smoke curl from the chimneys of scattered cabins.

A table, bountifully spread with vegetables from Leona's garden, held the decorated leg of lamb — the secret was out, it was goat.

Since Harold and Monroe had been Boy Scouts together in Chicago, they had some youthful escapades to remember from around the kitchen table on the second floor cold water flat in Chicago on Central Avenue.

My Father's booming laughter could be heard down the Chicago alley; and we joined in the hilarity with no clue as to the story, but just to be a part of Papa's humor.

"*Ja*, there was this farmer, Ole, from Norway, who had chickens who refused to lay eggs; the cow gave no milk. So he told his family that it was the wicked troll who lived in the mountains. Yes, it was the troll causing all the disasters; so he had a plan.

· · · · · · ·

"We'll all slip out in the wagon and leave secretly in the

night and we'll get far, far away from that old troll." So that is what they did. Quietly they put their belongings in the wagon and the horse pulled them far away from the scene of the disaster.

Well on their way, the farmer sighed with relief; but from the back of the wagon, the troll jumped up.

"Moving, are we?"

. . . .

(I can't believe it, that is fifty years old and we still tell it!)

Harold told about the time he was sitting with my father and several older ministers.

"Since I was just a seminary student, I didn't have much to say, but I remembered the humor these men expressed. I think it was Pastor Hansen who told of a dedication service in a Swedish church in Minnesota; many visiting pastors attended for this special day. There was this old Swede named Pete, who refused to attend church, but his wife coaxed until he came to the service. It was a hot day, and the pastor said, 'you men sitting next to the window, please open all the windows.'

"New farmer Pete was sitting next to a window that was stuck, but he drew himself up and gave a big push, drew his big belly in, then his pants fell down; so he flew head first out of the open window and ran to his wagon in his underwear; trousers left behind in the church. Needless to day, he never returned to church."

One of the other preachers told about a farmer who invited the preacher to dinner. About that time he heard a rooster crowing.

The farmer turned to the preacher and said, "You'd crow too if you had twelve sons in the ministry."

Then there was this preacher who said he never ate before preaching. After the service, someone asked the farmer how was the preacher's sermon? "Could just as well have et!"

As Papa's eldest daughter, I grew up listening to the same stories, but it was such fun to hear grown men laugh.

I remember one about the salesman who wanted to make a good impression on the farmer's young son since he was to share the same room; so when the boy knelt beside the bed, the salesman knelt at his side to pray.

"Don't know what you're doing mister, but the pot's on this side."

Monroe told how he met Leona at my Papa's church, and spent many hours in that kitchen drinking coffee.

I remember the day when Papa said, "Mama, no one has a big rocking chair in the kitchen. Come, Monroe, let's get this down to the basement." (Two flights of stairs.)

Mama said nothing, just poured coffee and sliced the bread.

The rocking chair was forgotten until one day when Uncle Barney came strumming his mandolin, striking up some fast polka music.

Papa jumped up and did some fancy steps while Mama's glasses slid down her nose. "Papa, do you think a minister of the gospel should be jumping around in the kitchen?"

"Probably not, Mama, but it sure is fun!" She laughed then sweetly said, "Now Bjarne and Monroe, do you think you could bring my rocking chair back to the kitchen?"

Papa had already forgotten that he had put it in the basement. "*O Ja*, that is a good idea."

So it came to pass that Mama's rocking chair again found its rightful place beside the "garbage burner" (small stove) in the kitchen, a warm place in winter.

Barney strummed his "worldly tunes" and Mama listened but when he winked at me and sang, "I'm coming back to you my hoola hoo" — The "hoola hoo" was a bit much for Mama, and when her glasses slipped down her nose, Barney knew it was time to switch to a Norwegian folk song.

It was from the rocking chair mama sang songs and told stories while she rocked the babies.

It was to the rocking chair we came when heartaches were too heavy to bear; here we would kneel and find rest for our soul. That is where I came when I was sixteen and the love of my life left me for the beautiful church pianist. Life was over!

Then I met Harold! Life was good!

"I remember that kitchen and rocking chair well," Leona spoke up with tears in her eyes.

"Baby Jeanelle, two weeks old, was dying. Dr. Thornton said, 'Now, Mama, you have five healthy children. Let this one go back to God.' His shoulders, stooped with weariness, the kindly doctor looked at Mama with compassion, sadly shook his head and descended two flights of stairs carrying his bag."

"Oh, I remember that day! I was sixteen years old, Leona, and you cried out, 'No, this baby must live.' I watched you rub her blue, lifeless body with hot olive oil, then put your finger down her throat, and you did a 'mouth to mouth' and sucked up the mucus and her color returned. Jeanelle lived to become a concert pianist, and was a joy to everyone around her, especially to Papa."

"It was then I was determined, more than ever, to become a nurse."

"I guess we could talk all night sharing stories from the past, but we need to get an early start in the morning to head toward Benton to spend another day with my folks before leaving for home, North Carolina!"

"I know my parents enjoy your visits," Harold continued, "and especially love those mountain stories!"

"We enjoy our trips to their home. Papa Jens doesn't say much, but the twinkle in his eye and his chuckle says, "It's time for another story." Leona added, "I'll bring some coffee and raisin cookies, so settle down for one of Monroe's 'Hettie Stories.'"

Monroe, the showman, took a bow!

. . . .

Now, this Miz Hettie, she done come out of the back mountains, same place where the spirit lives, in the crook of the live oak branch; yes sir, then she sets and casts spells, good spells, like 'whatever is good — think on that' — so she casts out good things on the wind, and tells secrets that the wind carries to Miz Hettie.

"It's a sure thing," says Hettie. "All kinds of messages come on the wind, even whispers of hope."

Once a year Hettie comes out of the mountains, gets all dressed up and puts on shoes, goes off to a Baptist conference where she comes back with tall tales she hears from preacher talk.

Now there was this big church, fancy it was, with a choir in long robes, and an orchestra, a real orchestra with fiddles, drums and trumpets — oh, it was fine.

There was this big baptizing night, with all the women in white and trousers and shirts for the men.

The fancy church had a big spotlight that shone on the river Jordan — not a real river, but a painting on the wall. But with the water in the tank and the light on it, why you'd think the river Jordan was fixing to roll — oh so beautiful, trumpets, choirs. Powerful it was!

There was this old fella, got his self borned again; wife been praying for him for years, and now it was time for him to get baptized; come out in all white, and they put the light on him. When he come up his wife hollered "hallelujah!" out loud in a city church — so happy she was.

Then there was this big woman, now let me tell you that mighty Jordan rolled, *Oh Roll Jordan Roll*, sure thought it would when she got in, the preacher had a time, yes he did; when the feet got down, the head come up, and when the head come down, the feet come up. Finally one big push and he got her under proper like for a good Baptist.

She got so excited, she grabbed the curtain to the old men's dressing room and pulled it, and the lights, right down on him — naked as a jay bird, bending over and hollering for his glasses.

Another old fella fell asleep through the whole baptizing, yes sir, sound asleep, but when he came to, it was all dark and he yelled out loud, "I'll be d@#%d if they didn't up and leave me."

All this in a fancy city church!

The choir kept singing *Shall We Gather at the River* and by that time I figured I'd rather have a river baptizing like that anytime, Lulla Belle got baptized in the creek and a snake slithered close by to see what was going on and the preacher yelled, "Satan get out of here!" That snake just slithered away.

We sang, *Shall We Gather at the River*, real powerful that day. Lulla Belle got under proper like.

Folks don't know what they miss when they don't go to meetin' — more things happen to make you cry and laugh in church, and I heard tell it's good to do both.

Seems like a lot of foolishness goes on, but Hettie says that the "Spirit" up in the live oak branch sends a message on the wind that says as long as the preacher sticks to the Word, it is powerful enough to get through the foolishness. She says the Word is forever settled, so I guess that settles it. I also heard on the wind that God likes to hear His children laugh.

Well ladies and gentlemen, that concludes the "Hettie Tales" for this time. Now we can thank God for the tears we've shed together but also for times of laughter.

Night had come to draw the shade of darkness over a sun-splashed day. Now it was time for sleep. When morning came, we turned our car down the mountain road to Benton.

· · · · · · ·

That was a long time ago and now they are all gone Home, but I can almost hear Barney's mandolin strumming his plaintive tune.

> *Sometimes I feel like a motherless child,*
> *A long way from home.*

I don't think my grandchildren will think the baptizing in the creek with the snake is funny, so I won't tell them, but somehow chuckling to myself makes the "long way from home" seem a little lighter.

I'll call my sister Joyce, instead!

Chapter Seventeen

The Mountain People

The visit from Monroe and Leona was like spring bursting forth in the middle of winter.

Mama Elise heard the old car rattle up the driveway, then the boisterous laughter of Monroe as he held Leona's hand to steady her steps. Even in her 80's, she still climbed mountain trails, and could decorate an old goat to look like choice lamb.

"Now, Sweetheart, take a little nap and I'll visit with the Jensens."

Gently he tucked a blanket around her frail shoulders, and stroked her face lovingly, "What an angel, the love of my life."

"We just came from a preacher's conference. One preacher got so carried away, he took off his coat; then loosened his tie and poor Sister Wilma wasn't too sure what else he'd discard. But then he got our attention when he shouted, 'Coming along the country roads on this beautiful day, I saw the farmers in the fields with their concubines. What a glorious sight to behold.'"

"Amen," shouted Sister Wilma. That was Papa Jens' favorite story.

"Don't you ever run out of stories, Monroe?" Mama asked.

"Oh no, Mama, life is full of stories. Most folks miss them because they don't realize that comedy in real life helps to balance the tragedy."

While Monroe spun his tales of their work in the mountains,

Mama Elise cooked fried chicken, mashed potatoes (with butter and cream), creamed peas and carrots (a favorite dish for Papa Jens and my Harold), and at the same time an apple pie was in the oven.

When Uncle Jack came home from work, within a short time, they were all seated around Mama's festive table, asking God's blessing on the food.

Leona, refreshed from her nap, entered into the lively conversation, and what a joy for her to sit down to a prepared meal when she usually cooked for others.

"One day we were coming down the mountain when the brakes failed. We kept going faster and faster. While Monroe was doing all he could to steer that old car, I kept screaming, 'Jesus, stop this car, Jesus, stop this car.' The car stopped!"

"It stopped against a tree, Leona."

"So, it stopped. Better than going over the edge to the ravine below."

"Come out on the porch," called Papa Jens. "Watch the sunset."

They rocked together in the cool of the evening and watched the display of color while daylight yielded to the shadows of night.

Monroe had another story.

. . . .

There was this preacher at a revival meeting ready to give an invitation and invite folks to get saved, baptized or join the church. To be sure someone would come, he included "rededication," all the time the choir sang softly, I Surrender All.

One by one they came and the evangelist asked, "Why do you come?"

"I come to join the church," or "I come for baptism;" then he turned to another one, "Well, sister, why do you come"?

"I come by bus, too far to walk."

That's about the time Papa Jens decided to go to bed, chuckling all the way.

. . . .

After a good night's sleep, and a Danish breakfast of delicate pancakes rolled up with fresh berries from Elise's garden, the tale bearer from the mountain prayed a blessing on the home that had became their "oasis in the desert," a Bethel to return to. It was their safe place where their weary bodies could be refreshed. Their bodies and minds were weary from the battle against ignorance, prejudice and a fear of "outsiders."

While they organized Sunday schools, they worked with the young people and inspired them to continue their education, and gave them hope for a brighter tomorrow. The women responded to the love and care Leona gave when their babies came, then slowly hope slipped in the cracks of doubt and they learned to use their homespun talent, and bring their quilts and crafts to the marketplace. The men watched when Monroe improved his cabin, then followed his lead.

It was a constant battle against "whatever will be will be," and "It was good enough for my Pappy, good enough for me."

Monroe's patience and good humor won the battle slowly as he worked with the men to improve their land.

Slowly, the mind that had been locked in a cultural mind set began to listen to the whispers from the heart.

When the children in Sunday school sang, "Jesus, Loves Me," the parents heard. When they sang "Soft like the voice of an angel comes whispering hope," the mountain people listened with their hearts.

Year after year, Leona and Monroe worked in the mountains. When they came down from the mountain, could be weeks or even months between visits, they brought laughter and sunshine to the Jensen home; but perhaps the Jensens never realized just how much they restored the souls of their mountain guests.

"Forget not His mercies," comes as a reminder from the Good Book and one of His mercies is the joy in the midst of life's tragedies when terrorists of hate seek to drown out love and take the song of the soul from a nation. It's the song of the soul that makes us stand tall after a crushing blow. Memories of past blessings renew faith for today and gives hope for tomorrow.

> *Not until each loom is silent,*
> *And the shuttle cease to fly,*
> *Will God unroll the pattern*
> *And explain the reason why?*
> *The dark threads are as needful*
> *In the weaver's skillful Hand.*
> *As the threads of gold and silver*
> *In the pattern he has planned.*
>
> — *Streams in the Desert* (selected)

· · · · · · ·

After the months of rain, sleet and muddy roads, spring burst forth in dazzling color and announced to the world that the blue birds of promise were on the way. The winter was past and the sound of spring came on the wind with whispers of hope.

It was time for Leona and Monroe to come down off the mountain for another visit.

Monroe's exuberant laughter rolled out of the car with him. Leona, smiling, confident, looked at him and smiled in amusement.

"Life would never be dull with that man."

The difference in their ages seemed insignificant in comparison to what they contributed as a team. Leona, twenty years older, stayed carefully in the background while she steadied the boat, managed the meager finances, turned their cabin into a model for the simple mountain people, and encouraged them in creative mountain talent.

Monroe, the enthusiastic preacher, with his joyous disposition and tireless energy, brought the mountain people to a place of trust in them, then to the Christ of the Cross. The mountain people had become accustomed to ignorance on fire with the thumping pulpit of hellfire and brimstone. Now they saw and heard truth in living color. Slowly the mountain folks moved closer to the flame of God's love.

Not only did Mama Elise and Papa Jens enjoy Monroe and Leona's visit, but it was also a time for them to give not only financially, but mental stimulation as well, with books, music and shared experiences. For everything there is a season, and into the ordinary routine this was a time for a burst of springtime that kept joyous laughter on the wind.

Once again Monroe was in rare form and the actor had a flair for the dramatic.

. . . .

There was this Miz Hettie, a mountain woman, who spun tales about ghosts and spirits that lived in the mountain holler.

Otto Ottis, from the feed mill, came out one morning and heard a kitten squalling in the feed store. "Scat! Scat."

But the cat didn't scat, even with a broom going after it. "Get out of my feed." That cat kept squalling until Otto kept looking around and there it was — not a cat, but a baby — wrapped in a blanket with a note. "Plez take ker of Moonbeam, borned in the corn field, Pa run off."

Well now, Otto didn't know what to do because he had no wife, but if Moonbeam came to his feed store, then he had to keep her.

About that time the strangest thing happened. A young woman from the other side of the mountain said, "Her man and baby gone, and she'd be glad to wet nurse the young-un. She also would be obliged, if she could find some work."

Otto said it was a sign, sure enough, that God Himself sent that young woman, and that Moonbeam took to her like a duck to water. When he saw Sallie Mae nurse that baby he got notions in his head, strange notions since he was an old bachelor, plumb foolishness. Sally Mae was only seventeen, pretty as a picture, big sad eyes and long black curly hair, didn't smile much and kept her head in a book to learn to read, but good at figures so Otto let her work at the mill.

One day, there was a barn dance planned, a real hoedown, and the fiddles were tuning up for the big Saturday night dance.

Sallie Mae looked shyly at Mr. Otto and asked, "Ever been to a hoedown?"

"No, never could figure out who'd go with me. Nope, I've never been."

"If someone went with you, would you go?"

"I reckon I would but who'd go with an old grizzly like me? Have you gone, Sallie Mae?"

"Oh no, Mr. Ottis, no one asked me, but if someone asked you, would you go?"

"I reckon I would, but who would ask me?"

"Would you go if I asked you? Cause no one asked me, so now I ask you?"

"Now why would a pretty young thing like you go with an old goat like me?"

"Cause you're the kindest man in the world, that's why."

You should have seen old Otto come to life, a haircut and shave, new overalls and a red plaid shirt, even new shiny boots. And that Miss Sally Mae got all dressed up in a flouncy skirt, and tied her hair back with a big red bow, and could they swing to the music! Some folks figured that she'd grieved long enough over her dead husband and baby.

Twas no time at all till a preacher come through these parts and there was a wedding. Then one year later that fine boy Otto Ottis was born and that was one proud Pa, called him "young Ottis." Folks around here say no one loves that pretty little Moonbeam like big Ottis did. She loved him too, and she played with little Ottis, then they both growed up.

Now they are gone! Young Ottis runs the feed store like his Pa did before he died. Then his Ma died. Folks said that Sally Mae was too young to die, but when old Ottis died, something died in Sally Mae. She loved him that much, and said that she wanted to sleep beside him in the church yard.

Now there is this fairy that lives in that big live oak tree down by the holler; she stays up in the crook of that big tree and looks out over the mountain and cast spells, good spells, on folks. She whispers to the wind; then the wind whispers the message to me. One day I heard the whispers in the wind that Sallie Mae was the mother of Moonbeam and that Ottis knowed it but wasn't about to ask fool questions that do no good. Some things best left for God to figure out.

Sallie Mae had done right by her baby. Now Moonbeam had a good education and married to a teacher. One thing about mountain folks, they don't tell on their own, and Moonbeam belonged to the mountain and never knew she was found in the feed store.

That's one of Hettie's latest stories from the mountain.

· · · · · · ·

Papa Jens called everyone to rock on the porch while Mama Elise brought out glasses of iced tea.

Jens, usually so quiet, spoke softly, "My mother's sister had a husband who disappeared. No one ever heard from him. The theory was that he had been kidnapped by a foreign country, since he was in the import-export business. My aunt died, never knowing what happened to him."

"In the meantime, she had children to support, so she began writing children's stories. She became quite successful and was able to educate her children and make a new life for herself."

They sat quietly and rocked, each returning to a far away memory, while spring came softly all around Mama Elise's gardens, buds peeking through to see if winter really left. Robins seemed to strut as the announcers of spring.

"Strange things happen that we don't understand." Mama Elise broke the silence. "I was told that my grandfather sailed the seas to India to buy precious spices. When he was home he had a special way of saying 'goodbye' or 'goodnight.' He would caress his wife's face tenderly, brushing her cheek with his hand, then kiss her and say 'goodnight' or if leaving on a ship, say 'goodbye.'

"One night, when the Captain was out at sea, my grand-mother sat in her rocking chair, knitting. She was startled by the Captain's presence; and he caressed her face gently, kissed her and said, 'Goodbye.' She jumped up! 'The ship has gone down! The Captain is lost at sea.'"

Leona listened quietly; then added, "God seems to use broken things and He makes a success out of earth's failures. All my life, I had my heart set on going as a missionary to China. My education was completed and the only thing left was a physical exam after the interviews. I was rejected because of a heart murmur and look how I have survived the mountain hardships. The man I loved went without me.

It was the dark valley of the soul, but I kept working as a nurse for several years and went through the trial of my faith and discovered that tragedy can turn to triumph. God makes us stronger than our circumstances.

Strange as our marriage might seem to some folks, God gave Monroe to me, and my strength was renewed, not only because of the joy of the Lord, but from the crazy, funny, con-tagious joy of my mountain man. It's all amazing grace. How fast the years pass. That was many years ago, and I am left to tell the story.

· · · · · · ·

> *You cannot change the past, but the past can change you, either for better or for worse. It all depends on how you look at it. The past can be a rudder to guide or an anchor to hinder. Leave your past mistakes with God and look to the future by faith.*
>
> — *With the Word*, Warren Weirsbe

• • • • • • •

Spring prepared the way for June to come on the scene, bursting out all over in color and sunshine. As the end of summer drew near, with all the camp meetings, and Sunday school picnics left behind, Leona and Monroe decided to come down the mountain for a visit before the October Homecomings took place. The old rattletrap died of old age and Monroe found a later model to show his friends.

After a delicious meal of fried chicken and apple pie, it was time to rock on the porch and watch the evening shadows chase the daylight behind the mountains. Papa Jens had watched the squirrels long enough. With a quiet chuckle, he asked, "Monroe, any more stories from the mountains?"

Monroe leaned back and waved his arms, while Leona dozed contentedly. She had heard these stories before.

• • • • • • •

Now there was this woman in Sleepy Holler who had twelve young-uns. She was getting on in years, 90, more or less, and Lizzie Mae lived with her daughter, Lula Belle.

Sister Lizzie Mae fell out one day, I mean fell out of the bed, at least Lula Belle found her on the floor. Lula Belle screamed for the ambulance, and Sister Lizzie Mae was on her way to the emergency room, siren blowing all the way.

By the time the ambulance reached the hospital, the word got out, and the Baptist church showed up with three preachers.

Lula Belle greeted them with, "Nary a word come out of her, in a coma. That's what it is."

When she was wheeled to her room, the nurses got busy putting some fool thing in her arm dripping water, and they put a hose under the sheet and whiskey dripped into the bottle, yes sir, looked just like whiskey.

Lula Belle asked all the preachers to pray for Momma; then told folks they could be expecting the biggest funeral this side of the mountain, cause Momma was in a coma, couldn't hear nothing, and probably getting a look at her mansion over the hilltop.

A young feller came in, looked like one of Jeb's grandkids, and needed a shave and a haircut. Said he'd been on call in the emergency room. He had a long white coat and some fool thing around his neck, looked like a big black snake. He said, "I have some questions to ask."

Wouldn't you think that with all that book larnin' he'd know enough now that he didn't need to ask questions.

"I've come to get her history."

That's when Lula Belle stood up. "History! All Sleepy Holler knows Momma's history; just look in the Baptist conference book and you'll see that every time the preacher needed a motion for something, has to do with Roberts Rules of Order, now who is Robert? But if there was a motion that needed doing, Momma shouted, "I move." That's a fact. It's in the book.

There was that time the preacher said we had to have a motion that we get a chandelier. Now let me tell you, that was the only time Momma didn't move. "I'm against it," she shouted. "No one knows what it is and no one can spell it, and besides we need a light fixture."

"What illnesses has she had?"

"Bit by a snake, but Pa put her foot in a cow plop, she done good."

"Her vital signs are good."

What do you know, that young feller believes in signs, and I told him that Momma did most everything by signs and I was mighty proud to think he'd say they are good; we knowed it all along. Right nice smile that young feller has, good teeth, too.

"Does she drink or smoke?"

Now let me tell you something, that's not a question you ask a good Baptist.

Nary a drop of whiskey touched my Momma's lips, but Pa has a still on the back 40. Momma don't know about that. A bit of snuff she like tolerable well, but cigarettes, never.

The Baptists from Sleepy Holler agreed. They also knew this would be the biggest funeral this side of the mountain.

Lizzie Mae was in a coma, so the plans were made around her bed.

Suddenly there was the sound of running feet coming down the hall. Sure enough it was Willie, the youngest son who missed Homecoming last year. No one misses Homecoming in Sleepy Holler — all Lizzie Mae's young-uns were there, all but Willie, that is. He got hisself a job in South Carolina and missed Homecoming; now his sins done found him out.

That rascal Willie just busted in, been drinking, he had, and hollered, "Momma, Momma, speak to me, I'm your baby boy, Momma."

"You hush, Willie. Momma's in a coma, can't hear nothing and don't come yelling around here. Get yourself some coffee. You know you missed Homecoming! Momma's in a coma cause she's mighty close to the pearly gates."

"Speak to me, Momma. I got a new red truck and I'm coming back to Sleepy Holler. Momma, just speak to me. I'm sorry I didn't get to Homecoming last year, but Momma I done come home now."

Let me tell you something. I seen a miracle, yes, sir, a real live miracle!

When Willie said, "I'm coming home," that tiny little woman, wrinkled like a prune, with her wispy hair in a knot on top of her head, well she sat straight up in bed. Yes, she did. I was there and I seen it. She sat straight up, almost as good as Lazarus coming out of that cave, she did. Sat up and said, "Willie take me home in that red truck. We gotta get ready for Homecoming."

The ambulance ride was good but that siren was the best! Whewwww!

When Homecoming came to Sleepy Holler, all the folks around showed up. Even the Methodists (who hadn't spoken to the Baptists for some time) forgot what they was mad about, 'cause now they had seen a real miracle.

Sunday morning, Lizzie Mae sat with all her young-uns and their young-uns. Willie sat beside her. The choir sang, "Coming home, coming home nevermore to roam. Open wide thine arms of love, Lord, I'm coming home." That's the day Willie came home!

Now, ain't that the best story you ever heard tell? But that's not all. The tables were filled with Methodist and Baptist casseroles, and side-by-side sat four-story high coconut cakes. Never in the history of Sleepy Holler had there been such a Homecoming.

As for Sister Lizzie Mae, she sat under a shade tree, dressed in her best and Willie brought her a sample of Baptist and Methodist dishes and she nodded her approval of all, not about to take sides; but a mite partial to Lula Belle's crisp watermelon pickles.

After a while, the musicians got ready for the all-night singing while the women cleared away the empty casserole dishes. Lizzie Mae sat back in her chair and tapped her foot to the music. Willie drew close and whispered in her ear, "Tell me, Momma, how close were you to the pearly gates?"

"Not too close, Willie, not too close."

She closed her eyes and rocked quietly, chuckling to herself. "Sure did hate to miss such a fancy funeral, but there will be another time."

"Momma, look, gotta stand up, 'cause everyone's joining hands to sing."

"Blest be the tie that binds our hearts in Christian love."

Now don't that beat all, Methodists and Baptists joining hands, makes one believe in miracles.

· · · · · · ·

Mama Elise laughed so hard she had to wipe the tears with her apron. Leona dozed through the story. Papa Jens said that it had been a good day and it was time to go to bed.

Tomorrow morning Mama Elise would have pancakes and berries, and she'd pack a lunch and put an envelope with the money in the basket.

Yes, it had been a good day.

Chapter Eighteen

The Farm

"Look at all these pictures!"

"I know. Sarah is getting albums organized because I get carried away and then can't get my writing done. It's so much fun to go back in time, almost like living your life all over again."

"Here's a picture of you and Papa. Where was this picture taken?"

"We are standing beside Thornapple Lake in Michigan, and I had a blue lace dress on. We had just announced our engagement. It was 1937, and then married in 1938."

"How in the world did you get to Michigan?"

"I might as well put my pen down Sarah, because that picture opens another story, Since you are here, Kathryn Elise, you might as well hear more about great grandmother Elise."

. . . .

Since I grew up with my Norwegian Mama I was able to get "on the scene" stories about your great grandparents and my parents. I was there. But it was difficult to get stories from Mama Elise. It was probably my own fault since I was intimidated, for too long by our "Queen Mary." I kept a safe distance until the last year when I had a deeper appreciation and greater understanding of her courage.

Some of the details come later from your Papa (my Harold) and your Uncle Howard. Uncle Jack seemed reluctant to speak of the past. But with the years come understanding and I could fill in the gaps.

Let me refresh your memory with the sequence of events. When Papa Jens refused to cross the ocean again, Mama Elise, Papa Jens and the two young children, Jack & Harriet, lived with Papa Jen's brother and family in Nebraska. Then Mama Jens found the advertisement for a manager of the banker's farm. Then Papa bought the Colorado farm that turned into a disaster, then they sold out and moved to Chicago. They put the money from the Colorado farm into a Chicago bank and the bank closed! They were penniless in a big city except that Jens had gone before them and had a bricklaying job. But all the money from years of hard work on the farms was gone! This was the depression!

This is when the Captain's daughter, once more, rose to the challenge.

She found a rent-free flat on Beach Avenue, near Humboldt Park, in return for maintaining the building.

For a moment, just imagine what it was like to leave the security of a safe place and become penniless in a big city!

Everyone was looking for work, Papa Jens laid brick, but soon family members who had lost jobs moved into the small flat. Papa Jen's younger brother, Uncle Sophus, came with his family. Then Harriet, the daughter, came with her husband Frank. A decision was made that Harold (your Papa) should leave high school and look for work. Howard and Fern, the younger daughter, remained in school, but Howard sold newspapers to help with finances. Fern helped to manage the household.

Harold found employment at Bunte Candy Company and was promoted to the personnel department. He also obtained a night watchman job for Jack. Each one contributed what they could, but it was Mama Elise who put her face to the wind of the new challenge. Harold and Jack packed a lunch and walked to work, and gave Mama their paycheck.

Poring over the newspaper want ads, Mama Elise found

one advisement for a nurse for an elderly woman. In her typical fashion, Queen Mary marched to the store and purchased a white uniform with white shoes, and applied for the job.

She was asked, "What are your credentials?"

Holding her head high, Elise answered, "I reared five children, managed a farm in Nebraska, cared for sick neighbors and animals. I believe I'm qualified for most anything."

Apparently the young Jewish man admired her "Hutzpah," or perhaps he was desperate at the moment. For whatever reason, she was hired on the spot to care for a difficult, strong willed, demanding mother. In that battle of wills, I could pick the winner! The Captain's Daughter!

In spite of feeding an overflowing household, Mama Elise kept a close account of the money until she came across a reduced sale of a run-down farm in Michigan. Pooling the resources, she was able to put a down payment on the neglected property, but she continued to care for her demanding patient, who in turn came to love her nurse and she learned to laugh again.

Mama Elise stayed with her patient until she died peacefully. Then her attention turned to the dilapidated farm that eventually became a place of thriving beauty with cattle, crops and lovely gardens. Once again, she chartered a course through the storm until the day came when Harold completed his education. Howard left the farm to become a banker; Uncle Jack stayed at the helm with Mama. He never quite had the courage to leave her, but then he may have known her better than anyone else did and thought she had suffered enough!

So now, my beautiful girls, you have heard how Papa and I had a picture taken at Thornapple Lake, close to the farm.

Years later, they sold the farm at a good profit and toured the South, looking for a place to plan retirement. They selected Arkansas with its rivers and mountains. Uncle Jack worked at *Reynolds Aluminum Company*. Papa Jens laid brick for special community projects —

especially for churches. Mama Elise became the Southern Lady with the Danish accent, and became famous for her garden tours. But no "feed sacks" for our Queen Mary!

Papa Jens and Jack adjusted to life as it was, not as they hoped it would be. We owe a great debt to Jack who lived out "honor father and mother" in an unselfish manner, but all the children honored them by living honorable lives.

It was in this setting that Joyce and I grew to love her. In turn she loved us, but always added, "You don't mind if I love Joyce more?"

With finances restored, the Captain's Daughter and her dashing architect from Copenhagen lived out a life of integrity and honor for 58 years. They went Home in peace, a life lived well.

After the sale of the Arkansas property, with an invisible "You can't go home again," Uncle Jack closed the door — he was alone.

He came to North Carolina to be near all of us and his home was filled with Danish art and Copenhagen china, but it was in the gardens, a showplace of beauty, that you could almost hear Mama Elise singing...

I come to the garden alone
While the dew is still is still on the roses.
And He walks with me, and
He talks with me.

My dear Sarah and Kathryn Elise, it's been a long story, and all those Mountain Tales were part of their lives in Arkansas. Uncle Jack watched you all grow up and now he, too, is Home. He died in his sleep — alone.

Uncle Howard took him to Benton, Arkansas, to be buried next to Mama Elise and Papa Jens.

You children have a rich heritage from remarkable people, not perfect, but with the courage to rise above the storms, hunch their shoulders, lean forward and face the wind.

It was time to close the door on another day. Sarah put the albums away and Kathryn Elise asked for another story. That story would come another day.

· · · · · · ·

Only once did I get a glimpse into what might have been a secret corner of Mama Elise's heart. It was on one of our special visits to Arkansas.

One early morning, Mama Elise and I enjoyed a walk through her lovely garden and I watched her talk to her flowers. "Now there, you need a little dressing." "Oh my, so you decided to open up this morning, my beautiful rose — how lovely!"

I followed, listening and watching, and learned my love of gardening from her.

Later, we sat on the swing and watched the butterflies and with a faraway look she spoke, as though to herself. "I made a place of beauty out of the banker's farm. Yes, I did, then looked away. Her white hair framed a still beautiful face with classic features. Her slender hands lay folded on her aproned lap. It was her blue eyes that seemed to travel back in time, not seeing me, but looking into a long ago time.

· · · · · · ·

"He came to check the animals." That's what he said. But he always accepted an invitation to lunch, until that lunch became a part of our day.

Papa was gone all day, laying brick, and when he came home he was too tired for conversation, but enjoyed a good meal and the quiet of the evening, alone with his thoughts. I really only had Jack to talk to, but he was at school and the younger ones played.

It was pleasant to have someone to discuss the books I brought from the library and to get the town news and he enjoyed the gardens and knew the names of the plants. He said it was refreshing to leave the musty bank and walk with me in the garden; then enjoy a delicious lunch made by the best cook in the county. Yes, that's what he said, Margaret, "the best cook."

One day he said he could never understand how someone so young and beautiful could manage the farm like I did. I gathered some vegetables for him to take home; then I picked the most beautiful flowers in the garden to take to the bank for him and the others to enjoy.

That was all, Kathryn Elise, it was like a gate closed to a secret garden.

Now they are all gone!

It was a moment that came and left and never returned. It was the silence that said more than words and one day, when I sat on my patio and watched the birds in the bird bath and looked over my garden (that came from the cuttings of her garden) my own heart seemed to fill in the stories from the silence.

I tried to picture myself on the day the banker said "goodbye." Mama Elise's safe place had been taken away and she was on her way to the unknown Colorado because of Papa Jen's impulsive decision. (I wonder what might I have done?)

Sometimes, my dear, there can be a deep friendship that goes beyond words. I'm afraid that your generation misses the value of true friendship, a friendship that stays within the fence of God's protective laws.

For Mama Elise I believe it was something like that. For her, if it meant sitting across the table knowing that someone believes in you, just a look of admiration. It was reaching for a work-worn hand and saying, without words, "you are beautiful." It can be a sign, a deep sign, almost a sob that says, "I'll hold you in my heart for always." That is all — no words, no arms to embrace, no kiss to remember, just a sign. That kind of friendship goes beyond the changeable emotions and fills an empty place in the heart — a place that says you are valued by someone for your worth.

I believe that our Mama Elise, when it came time to say goodbye, that she conveyed, without words, but with blue eyes misty with tears, "thank you for giving me the chance to be Captain Mogenson's Daughter."

The banker could have taken her hand in his and said with his heart through his eyes, "Thank you for making the garden bloom, not only on the farm, but also in my heart."

Perhaps she gave him a rose to press in his Bible. Years later, just maybe, there would be a young child who would say, "Papa, why is this flower in your Bible?"

"It's a rose from a long ago time, a long time ago."

· · · · · · ·

It was time for my Kathryn Elise to return home. She had her story and there would be another day. I wanted to call out, "The past is gone forever, but hope for the future belongs to you."

I put my papers aside and looked out into my garden where Mama Elise's dessert-gold Iris was about to pop open.

"I'm sorry it took so long for me to learn to love you, but you were intimidating, Queen Mary. No, I don't mind if you love Joyce more."

I closed the door.

Chapter Nineteen

From Tears to Triumph

With a cup of coffee in my hand, I reached for the morning paper. Headlines screamed, "Another Suicide Bomber."

Everything inside me wept as I sat down to write with pen in hand. Unable to put down words, the hours flew by until the day was almost to the place where shadows slip in to chase daylight behind the mountains.

A walk by the ocean was what I needed — where the waves roll in and the waves roll out; where seagulls cry in the wind; and where grains of sand slip through my fingers like the hours had slipped through my day.

It was all the same as last year when the waves rolled and the seagulls cried. But, that was before Ground Zero and suicide bombs.

Within a few weeks, I'll walk through the path with the tangled bushes and yellow Tiger Lilies, then up the wooden steps bringing supplies to replenish the empty cupboards at the beach house.

Somehow, I sensed that we as a family need more than replenished cupboards. If my soul feels empty, barren, drained by tears of sorrow, how do the others feel coming across the miles to be refreshed at the beach house? Today, I weep alone, not only for the world, our nation and our courageous leaders, but I also weep for our churches that seem to have a hole in the soul. I weep, not only for America's families, but for my own family, especially the young ones. When they look to me with searching eyes, what do I, the "old and wise," have to say?

"Oh, Lord, it's not my brother or my sister, but it's me, oh Lord, standing in the need of prayer."

It comes again, the music of the past — a rudder to guide or an anchor to hinder, that feather of hope on the wings of a song.

I was back for a moment in my Father's Norwegian church in Chicago. I heard the music — as a child growing into teen years — the choir, a sprinkle of fifteen voices — but I heard a cathedral choir. Mr. Nelson's bass singing, "The rolling mighty sea," and Leona holding them all on the key with "Wonderful Grace of Jesus" — it all made the wonderful grace of God roll like the ocean.

Now, I needed to hear again about that grace that rolls like the sea. I needed a reminder of that faith that must keep me today, since I can't stop weeping for the mothers, with empty arms around the world.

When I visited Israel, I asked Jimmy, our Christian Arab guide, "Will there be peace?"

"Not until the Prince of Peace returns; but we must keep trying. If I don't see you on earth, I'll meet you at the Eastern Gate."

That's what the string band played in Papa's church. I can see them now when Papa announced. "*Ja*, now we will hear from the string band."

About twelve came from the back of the church, walking slowly to take their "places in the sun," tuning up their guitars, mandolins and zither and waiting for Mr. Lundaman to lead with his violin bow. They played and sang.

> *I will meet you in the morning*
> *Just inside the Eastern Gate*
> *Then be ready faithful pilgrim*
> *Lest it be too late.*

They never seemed to start together or end together, but the music kept coming back through the years. It was different to tell if they sang Norwegian or English, but the song was heard.

That was long before the Towers fell and we heard about Ground Zero. We can't go back and repeat time, but we can learn that the precious moments of life cannot be put off. Going through the pictures with Sarah and the albums, I was given a new perspective of family stories that relay truth from one generation to another. I don't have many years left, but I have molten moments to fill with his grace and hope. I need to keep rolling these into the next generation, to sustain the steps of those who follow my steps in the sands of time.

> *How much I owe to*
> *Love so Divine*
> *Love so Sublime*
> *Love that is deeper than any sea*
> *Love for us all — how can it be?*

I owe a debt to those who were before me, who received that love divine and lived out the grace of God in simple everyday living.

Whenever I watch the sun cast the last rays over the waves that keep rolling in and rolling out I am reminded that —

> *There is a tide in the affairs of men*
> *which taken at the flood, leads on to fortune;*
> *Omitted, all the voyage of their life*
> *is bound in shallows and in miseries.*
> — Shakespeare, *Julius Caesar*, Act 4, scene 3

I don't want to be in the shallows, let me ride the waves of God's Grace, sufficient for each new day. Before the curtain of night covers me in sleep, I quietly ask God to "guide, teach, instruct." Then morning slips in to remind me of a new day.

My sister Grace said at one time: "Margaret, you see the family through rose-colored glasses; I see black and white."

Years later she added, "Your way is better; not rose-colored glasses, but the lens of love."

I was there when my sister Grace was born at Christmas time, December 23, 1919. We were living in Brooklyn, N.Y. in *Bestemor's* (grandmother's) flat. Bernice, my 2 year old sister, and I were inseparable — slept together, played together until I had to go away.

All I remember about that day is that I was bundled up and taken away and placed in a high crib in a glass cubicle. I was almost four years old. I couldn't reach my father who stood outside the cubicle, in a long black coat, boots and fur hat, gloves in his hand, and a very white, sad face. I tried to reach out to him to hold me, but he shook his head as I stood in a long white hospital gown.

I had diphtheria!

Before me, even now, I can see my father's sad face and I recall thinking, "I must not cry!" I watched him walk down the hall. He came day after day to stand in his long black coat and looked so sad until the day came when he wrapped me up in a blanket and took me home. Once again my sister Bernice and I were together. *Bestemor* made *Jule Kake* and I was there to hear a newborn baby's cry. It was Grace. Bernice sat on Papa's lap to dip a piece of *Jule Kake* in his coffee — *godt* (good). "Mama, Bernice is so hot!" She was wrapped in a blanket, and taken away, as I had been, but Bernice didn't come home again! On a wintry New Year's Day, three men stood together — Papa, Uncle Joe and Pastor Hansen — beside on open grave in freezing snow and wind.

"Let not your heart be troubled."

"The Lord is my Shepherd." The wind carried the words over the small casket. Papa kept hearing the words, the same words he heard in Norwegian as a young child, when his family died — so much sorrow, so much death. "I must preach more about Heaven," he said. "*Ja*, life has too many sorrows."

"Come, come," Uncle Joe urged. "We must go home now."

"No, no oh no, I can't leave her alone in the cold. The wind is so cold."

"She is safe now. There is no wind and she is warm. It's time to go now for a cup of coffee."

They came together in long black coats, leaving the lonely grave in the wind with no flowers — too cold! *Bestemor* was there to serve hot coffee and *Jule Kake*. I helped *Bestemor*.

Papa went to his study where no one was allowed to touch his priceless books, all in perfect order, and then he saw where Bernice had poked the books with her little hands to be uneven. Papa sat down and wept.

"Papa, did you put the socks on?"

"*Ja*, I put the woolen socks on her and wrapped her in a blanket."

Mama turned her face to the wall and wept from a broken heart. *Bestemor* came in with baby Grace. "Come, turn around and nurse the living. Life goes on!"

I stood by the window and looked up into the starry sky, "Mama, God just made an exchange. He took Bernice but gave us Grace" — and Mama was comforted.

· · · · · · ·

There was another time when Mama wept. She was only 4 years old, living in Norway. She watched her mother (our *Bestemor*) walk down the road sobbing, leaving Ella (my Mother) and Uncle Joe behind. She was leaving for America!

"*Mor, Mor*," (Mama). I ran after her but she kept walking. The aunt said, "Don't call her *Mor*, call her Tilda!"

Ella stood tall and said "*Min Mor*" (my mother).

A neighbor said, "Who does she think she is?"

"She's a Lund. That's who she is — a Lund!"

My Mama remembered it well. Then she, too, came to America at 15 years of age.

It was Jeanelle, my youngest sister, who found our mother sobbing her heart out after *Bestemor's* funeral.

I never heard such heart — rending sobs, like she was that young child again, crying for her lost mother. I just waited, then took her in my arms and said, "Mother, God was so good to let you be near her all these last years, both you and Uncle Joe. Think of all the joy you gave her. Now she is Home — no more misunderstanding — she is safe!"

Before our Mama died, Harold, my husband, was sitting beside her one night so I could sleep and he heard her call out like a young child, "Mor Mor," like that little four-year-old calling for her mother. Perhaps that's why she had such a mother's heart for broken people around her. Out of the past we learn again that earth has no sorrow that Heaven cannot heal.

The proud Captain Mogenson heard D.L. Moody preach about God's amazing grace. He bowed his head and heart and became a child of God and Founded a Seaman's Mission for the seafaring sheep and led them into the fold of God's Love.

Mama Elise, who believed that "God helps those who help themselves," came to that place when she heard Dr. DeHahn preach about God's grace over Chicago W.M.B.I. Moody Station. She bowed her proud head and changed her motto to, "I can do all things through Christ."

The ocean of God's grace rolls from generation to generation and the mending yarn to heal the broken hearted and give a shining hope, is the thread of love.

How is it possible that hate can lash with raging fury against the helpless and leave such heart-breaking destruction in its path?

Then again, how is it possible for God to so love the world that He gave His Son and allowed Him to be lashed by the fury of hatred, and to take our place, so that if we believe in Him, we receive the gift of eternal life.

It is to the cross we come with our broken hearts, broken dreams, broken promises; and it is at the cross where God's arms of love reach for us to mend the hole in the soul with the golden thread of life held in his nail-pierced hands.

It is to the empty tomb that we come to cry out, "Because

he lives, I can face tomorrow."

It is when we bring the "Ground Zero" of life to the foot of the cross that from the tears of tragedy will come the triumph of the soul.

It is time to lift up our heads and know that our Redemption draws near. We can almost hear the footsteps of the coming King when every knee shall bow and every tongue confess that Jesus is Lord.

> *And he shall reign forever and ever*
> *King of Kings and Lord of Lords.*

Hallelujah!